Growing Old—
The Ultimate
Freedom

BOOKS BY MAXWELL JONES, M.D.

Social Psychiatry: A Study of Therapeutic Communities.
  Tavistock Publications (1952)
The Therapeutic Community. Basic Books (1953).
Social Psychiatry. Charles C. Thomas (1962).
Beyond the Therapeutic Community. Yale University Press
  (1968).
Social Psychiatry in Practice. Penguin (1968)
Maturation of the Therapeutic Community. Human Sciences
  Press, Inc. (1976).
The Process of Change. Routledge & Kegan Paul (1982).

Growing Old— The Ultimate Freedom

Maxwell Jones, M.D.

INSIGHT BOOKS
HUMAN SCIENCES PRESS, INC.
72 FIFTH AVENUE
NEW YORK, N.Y. 10011-8004

Printed in the United States of America
987654321

Library of Congress Cataloging-in-Publication Data

Jones, Maxwell.
  Growing old, the ultimate freedom.

  Bibliography: p.
  Includes index.
  1. Retirement.   2. Old age.   3. Spiritual life.
4. Death.   I. Title.   [DNLM: 1. Aging—psychology.
2. Quality of life.   Retirement.   WT 30 J78g]
HQ1062.J65   1988   305.2′6   87-22787
ISBN 0-89885-405-9

Contents

Introduction

The aim of this book is to question the validity of many of our Western cultural stereotypes regarding the process of growing old. At the most fundamental level is that growing old presages death, which for most people is a frightening prospect, one which is not studied and discussed—as it should be if we are to be at least somewhat prepared for this eventuality.

In a similar way we tend to view retirement from a routine job as an unpleasant topic instead of as a time to look back on life and to build on the positive areas of interest that were previously sacrificed to the god of work. Just as planning for a holiday is often as exciting and fulfilling as the experience of the holiday itself, so the wisdom of a positive attitude toward our later years, starting at an early age, may pay a handsome dividend in terms of interest and purpose.

Another issue that is raised repeatedly in this book is the importance of our latent spirituality. Many people are aware that we are part of something infinitely greater than our individual selves, but we seem to lack the incentive or the encouragement to seek in this direction despite a vast recent literature on this subject.

These are three considerations that explain the title of this book, *Growing Old—The Ultimate Freedom*. I am using the title to convey a serious message and not as a passport to heaven or as a paradoxical catch phrase.

I have to admit that in comparison with many others, life has been kind to me and circumstances have conspired to push me ever further along a process of growth toward an inner awareness. I have never lacked interest or enthusiasm in relation to all stages of my childhood and working life. Nor have I known real hardship either financially or environmentally. Eleven years ago, to my complete surprise, I suffered a coronary infarct, followed by major heart surgery, which I barely survived. Despite considerable curtailment of my physical output, I have nevertheless experienced more interest and excitement than ever before.

To illustrate one stage of this slow process of change and personality growth as I see it, I think of the time when I was the Medical Director of Dingleton Hospital near Edinburgh from 1962 to 1969. During that time, my colleagues and I established a model of a democratic system or *therapeutic community* in a mental hospital that achieved a world-wide reputation and proved to us the value of an open system over any other social organization for a mental hospital.

The social structure of a therapeutic community is characteristically different from the more traditional hospital. The term implies that the whole community of staff and patients is involved, at least partly, in treatment and administration. The extent to which this is practicable or desirable will depend on many variables, including the attitude of the leader and the other staff, the type of patients being treated, and the sanctions afforded by higher authority. The emphasis on free communication in and between both staff and patient groups and on permissive attitudes that encourage free expression of feeling imply a democratic, egalitarian rather than a traditional hierarchical social organization (Jones, 1976).

However, since leaving full-time work more than a decade ago, I have wondered increasingly about what the mental health profession calls treatment. Vast amounts of money are spent on patients' fees as well as on staff salaries and, more recently, lawyers' fees without openly questioning our whole philosophy of treatment. This meant that although I'd enjoyed a relatively successful hospital experiment, I now began to question the whole philosophy pertaining to mental health facilities.

At the same time we are preparing youth through school, college, and on-the-job training for programmed roles at university and the job market. Again, there is relatively little examination of our philosophy reflected by our behavior in the Western world and the threat to both humanity's survival and to the world ecology while we continue our materialistic way of life as usual. I see much the same generic problem facing the areas of treatment, education, and industry in our Western world and question their appropriateness.

One alternative that might be considered to have equal validity in all three areas would be to pay more attention to human relations, which in general we seem to leave to chance. This change would entail a new significance accorded to group interaction between people in all walks of life so that everyone would come to realize the need for a support system that could be trusted and turned to as required. I see this as everyone's responsibility. If I had not experienced this phenomenon in many forms and in many places, I'd be highly skeptical, but I know the value of a supportive environment in virtually all age groups, including schools, universities, prisons, hospitals and industry. This concept will be elaborated upon throughout the book, with particular reference to the elderly.

Interest in the paranormal is growing rapidly, thanks to the new interest in Eastern philosophies, New Age thinking, and the impossibility of proving many of our basic beliefs about

God, religion, subatomic theory, evolution, and so on. Many thoughtful people now believe that to be normal may also include some mystical and unprovable beliefs, and thus may transcend the familiar objective reality of the past. It is in this context that in this book I talk about body, mind, and spirit, not only in relation to our individual selves but also in trying to understand different levels of consciousness that we tend to ignore even when, for example, they obtrude into our dreams. This interest leads to the concept of a universal consciousness of which we are probably an inherent part.

As an indication of the changing climate of opinion regarding paranormal experiences, it is worth mentioning that a recent poll done by the National Opinion Research Center of the University of Chicago showed that 67 out of 100 Americans claim to have experienced extrasensory perception at some time in their lives. (*Brain/Mind Bulletin*, 1987).

I am now free to live my life as I please, having slowly withdrawn from the rat race of professional life as a psychiatrist and social ecologist. My interest in group and community work has moved from hospitals to the general community. My previous focus on people has now transgressed the boundaries of the human body and mind to include the spirit, which is in turn a part of the energy emanating from the environment as a whole. So now the question is, who am I? A separate physical entity or just a part of the dance of the electrons? Maxwell Jones or a tiny bundle of energy somehow linked to a universal pattern through a Supreme Being or God?

Perhaps we should stop using the word *retirement* with all its negative connotations, and use instead the concept of *freedom*. Freedom to read, to interact socially and to learn; freedom to change one's lifestyle and set priorities based on contemplation and absence of social pressures; freedom to question cultural stereotypes or the politics of fear and greed. Freedom to stand back and realize the growing loss of credibility afflicting the world of politics on local, national, or international levels and the lessening public confidence in medicine, law, economics, banking, and education. Freedom to explore absurd ideas, fantasies, and dreams that may in time come to reflect the limitations of our current concept of reality. What a challenge for thinking people everywhere—and especially for those of us who are relatively free to ponder without restrictions of time and expediency. Where did we go wrong in our Western culture, and what can be done now before it is too late?

In the following synopses of each chapter of this volume, I raise five topics of particular relevance to the elderly and their place in a possible brave new world:

CHAPTER 1: RETIREMENT AS FREEDOM

For most people, their lifestyle up to the time of freedom (retirement) has been largely a matter of conformity—following the guidelines expected by parents, the peer group, educators, religion, employers, and so on. Schooling, reading and other forms of enquiry may widen people's horizons through increased knowledge. Only in recent decades has our Western culture included aspects of Eastern philosophies that widen our global perspective and help us to consider less materialistic goals.

Work in therapeutic communities has resulted in a democratic process we call *social learning* or *process learning* in the hope that it may lead to change in the direction of a more open and holistic view of life. To be optimally effective this process of learning requires periodic exposure to a supportive and highly motivated peer group, as for instance in a temporary residence in a center for learning about drug and alcohol addiction, personal growth, old age, or mysticism, with frequent discussions to look at and compare individual lifestyles and interpersonal differences. With the help of a professional facilitator experienced in group dynamics and social systems theory and practice, sufficient trust may develop to risk exposing inner personal feelings to the group. We come to see ourselves through the eyes of other group members. As individuals, we discuss the unfamiliar or controversial and incorporate new and congenial ideas. In this way, we widen our perspective on life's problems, and through social interaction learn for ourselves and widen our understanding of life: a process I have called social learning.

In addition, we ourselves must change our own self-awareness, our understanding of who we are and why we are alive, instead of accepting passively the conformist attitudes, values, and beliefs of our success-oriented Western society. Can we, as older people freed, at least in part, from a conformist culture, make a significant contribution toward a world where understanding and compassion transcend the materialistic and technological outlook threatening our very existence?

This subjective synopsis summarizes my own use of the freedom of old age: to seek what is to me the meaning of life. Everyone must explore his or her options in respect to the optimal use of the freedom afforded by our later years, always bearing in mind that for some people less fortunate, mere survival replaces any luxury such as freedom of choice.

CHAPTER 2: EDUCATION FOR LIFE

The pursuit of knowledge in terms of teaching as a predominantly one-way process from teacher to student is the primary focus of our educational system from primary school to university and beyond. This still leaves relatively untouched what we call social learning and personality growth. It also excludes, to a large extent, such issues as the meaning of a purposeful and fulfilling life, fostering our latent creativity, exploring the transcendental, and the unique problems of old age and the process of dying.

There is another problem area that seems to be largely overlooked in our educational system. As children we all have experienced a rich fantasy life, but our culture and education have impressed us with the importance of being "realistic," and these early abstract mystical trends have usually been stamped out—except perhaps for those lucky ones who managed to find a career in the world of art. But relics of this inner awareness are still manifest in adult life, as dreams, intuition or interest in the supernatural, the spiritual, and so on. The question is, how can we begin to recapture this latent potential which our culture and its preoccupation with conformity to realistic standards of learning and behavior has repressed over a lifetime?

If an open system is encouraged in places of learning, then both *teaching* or the transmission of knowledge from teacher to class, and the interaction implicit in *social learning* or learning as a social process, are possible. This opportunity for social learning could be introduced in education from elementary school onward.

Although there is some evidence to suggest that some schools are adopting more open systems and social learning, it will be a long time, if ever, before this approach is part of education in general. In the meantime, there is no reason why such an approach should not become an inherent part of the ultimate freedom of old age. Loneliness so common in old age is being met in part by many social agencies, but as in the case of various residential facilities, social learning through interaction in a group setting is a rarity.

CHAPTER 3: COMMUNITIES AS SUPPORT SYSTEMS

One of the factors in the decline of Western civilization to the present crisis of survival is the relative disappearance of family life and especially the old extended families. This trend is bound to be further affected, with the growth of the feminist movement resulting in equality of opportunity for women in industry and the social services (including health, etc.). The problems of two-career families have to be balanced against the computer age with a diminishing job market, vividly portrayed by the fate of many recent university graduates unable to find work. Linked with these evidences of social dislocation is the unsettlement of youth, ranging from school dropouts to the surge of drug addiction, alcoholism and the loss of a positive purpose in life.

There is growing awareness among all age groups that everyone needs a support group. To segregate the age groups, the races, or the unwell and disabled is a phenomenon of our age and, except in special circumstances, is both unproductive and dehumanizing. The basic factor is that isolation engenders fear and paranoia, and throughout recorded history the tribal or social instinct in one form or another has been used to counter the vulnerability of the individual. In this age of social upheaval and fear of survival, the disintegration of our social lives calls for new patterns of social integration or support that reaches its height in old age.

CHAPTER 4: DEATH, DYING, AND THE AFTERMATH

At first, to say anything about dying seems absurd or at best presumptive. And yet at a subjective level, I feel I am already in transition. The relative freedom from commitment that many if not most elderly enjoy would seem to offer an opportunity for some serious thought about the subject of death. To me, this long-term perspective affords an exciting adventure into the unknown. As I sit in my office contemplating the view of a tree-covered slope and the effortless gliding of birds— hawks, gulls, and ravens—responding to upward currents of air, I too feel uplifted. This familiar feeling of harmony with nature has stirred the imagination of countless poets and artists, but it also usually engenders both joy and awe in anyone willing to pause, look and wonder—a surrender to the inscrutability and mystical quality of life, and an intuitive awareness of something bigger than we can experience consciously. This is part of the ultimate freedom referred to in the title of this book. No matter how much suffering, hopelessness, and frustration have been a part of an active working life, the freedom of later life can open the door to the beauty of the world all around us.

My aim in this book is to demonstrate the possibility of rediscovering our latent potential for spiritual growth and a feeling of being a part of an infinitely greater whole. Such a search for the Holy Grail would seem to have a particular relevance in our latter years.

CHAPTER 5: SPIRITUALITY

This for me was by far the most difficult chapter to write and I have never overcome my feeling of utter unimportance. Luckily for me, the literature is rich in this field, and here I found solace: "We wait on the Lord, either to feel him in words, or in silence of spirit without words, as he pleaseth", wrote a prominent Quaker in the 17th century (Kenworthy, 1979).

The subject of egotism has caused me endless trouble. I seem to have no capacity to identify with Buddhist philosophy, particularly the goal of selflessness. In my lifelong struggle against the abuse of power in favor of a democratic system, my colleagues and I have of necessity needed to have a strong belief in ourselves, especially when at times we seemed to have the whole medical profession out to destroy us (Jones, 1982). As time wore on, and as we survived numerous official enquiries and found a growing support in some quarters, a feeling of fulfillment emerged that I cannot separate from ego satisfaction. Is this egotism neutralized by our open social system and willingness to listen to criticism in order to learn and change?

This ego problem seemed to lessen as the interest in group work became increasingly spiritual.

On a more general scale, there seems to be a strong spiritual trend running through many facets of life, including politics. In Europe, the Green politics ask what the purpose of economic growth is if it progressively destroys our ecology and leads to disaster for future generations. Almost one in ten West Germans voted Green in the last election. The movement is gaining ground rapidly in Europe and the U.K., while in Canada and the U.S. concern for the environment is high on the polls as an election issue. In some religions, a similar holistic and global trend is emerging and bringing spiritual values into everyday life. These and other spiritual issues are discussed in Chapter 5.

A few impressions have been paramount in my quest. First, to seek after truth (although truth means different things to different people), means for many people to seek something absolute and beyond our comprehension, but something that nevertheless represents the ultimate reality. Next, in contemplation, there may come a feeling of exaltation with or without a definitive alteration of consciousness such as an awareness of a bright light or even an image. Usually I'm aware that my breathing is deeper, and a surge of energy accompanies the joyousness, and I'm an active seeker again. Another impression is that an increasing number of college-age people are motivated to turn away from the temptations of money, power, and greed, and to seek instead lives dedicated to the betterment of humankind.

1

Retirement as Freedom

For most people, their lifestyle up to the time of freedom (retirement) has been largely a matter of conformity—following the guidelines expected by parents, the peer group, educators, religion, employers, and so on. Schooling, reading and other forms of enquiry may widen people's horizons through increased knowledge, but they do relatively little to prepare young people for the problems of living.

This sounds very pompous and opinionated, but it is at least my honest opinion. In any case, if I am to get my message across at all then I must at all costs avoid being diplomatic or insincere. Like many other eighty-year-olders who have followed a particular belief system over a lifetime, I have evolved certain theories, which have been expressed in scores of articles in the medical press and in books, and are, I think, highly relevant to the problems of aging. For most people who have "enjoyed" full-time work, retirement may mean the partial disappearance of a peer group. This peer group at work may not have included deep friendships that extended into ordinary social life, but nevertheless the loss may be keenly felt. For me, since leaving full-time hospital work in 1974 I have become painfully aware that absence does *not* make the heart grow fonder. There is an entirely understandable and healthy tendency for the staff to regroup after the loss of a leading figure and to find a new identity they can call their own. When I visit the original therapeutic community near London that pioneered the concept of an open system in a hospital, I feel something of an interloper. The present director is a friend whom I have known from the days of my tenure there (1947–1959), but apart from him I know no one. The culture is still familiar as a therapeutic community, but it has changed to the extent that I no longer *know* it. So I really am an interloper in *their* hospital. Moreover, they want to describe *their* achievements largely without reference to the past. I respect this truth as an important aspect of their collective self-image, but it still leaves a vacuum for me—and just a little pain at the reminder that I'm a has-been.

Most people in their later years would probably stress loneliness as their biggest single problem, particularly if they are single. This brings home the sad fact that we have no alternative but to accept our own responsibility for achieving some form of social network to improve the quality of our lives. I doubt if anyone really seeks to be alone most of the time. Unfortunately merely keeping busy may not compensate for this feeling of loneliness and relative insignificance.

The Everyone-Seems-to-be-Busy-but-Me Syndrome

One rather subtle aspect of loneliness is the realization that everybody seems to be busy but me. I am blessed with a wonderful wife, but she has a very demanding career to attend to, and although we chose to have no children, we seem to spend less time together than before my retirement. I know that this is a distortion of the objective reality—and how exceptionally fortunate I am compared to most men of my age. Even so, my very freedom to spend my days as I choose creates a subjective feeling of neglect that I despise in myself. Everyone I know seems to be busy with their work, their children or their other interests. The fact that I feel like a spoiled brat does not help, and I even begin to envy our golden retriever dog whom my wife adores! Had I been less fortunate, I can see how easy it would be to become sorry for myself and, to use a common expression, have a chip on my shoulder.

This everyone-seems-to-be-busy-but-me syndrome can lead to a more serious state of mind. Loneliness with its accompanying loss of perspective can develop into what is often called *paranoia*—a term borrowed from mental health literature in order to indicate a state of mind that can be described as an illness. Ordinary events can become subjectively distorted, and unwarranted suspicion can lead to delusions that can have serious consequences for the individual and for others in his social network.

Like many other people, I see the need to anticipate such possibilities and to be ready to discuss openly these and other pitfalls associated with the process of growing old. Again, it seems to me that everyone in this older age bracket has to assume the responsibility to become associated with a social network of some kind and, if necessary, to create such a group by one's own efforts. To keep busy is not enough, nor are pastimes such as bingo, bridge, and bird watching. Without opportunity to interact with similar-minded people, irrespective of age, we run the risk of losing our sense of perspective, which in our younger years was an automatic accompaniment to our social life at work, at play, and even the fleeting contacts that occur when traveling or shopping.

It is well known that irrespective of age, no one can retain his ordinary state of mental balance when subjected to an experimental experience known as *sensory deprivation*. This is a situation wherein as far as possible the volunteer is deprived of the usual sensations of hearing, seeing, feeling, smelling, and touch. Insulated from these sensations from the outside environment, which are essential as reminders of an objective reality and a personal identity, anyone is liable to become confused, bewildered, and terrified to a point approaching what we choose to call insanity. This extreme example shows the importance of maintaining a social network and interaction with other people as an aspect of health, much like the diabetic needs a maintenance-dose of insulin to retain biological balance.

This amounts to a self–imposed prescription to enter into some form of frequent social interaction where one can feel a degree of security, and also have the opportunity to help other people through dialogue and help oneself at the same time.

SELF-HELP THROUGH SOCIAL INTERACTION

In the following two chapters of this book I shall be elaborating on the many positive potentials inherent in any voluntary group of motivated people who derive understanding and energy from social interaction in a group setting.

For many, perhaps the majority of people who have led routine and somewhat monotonous lives, there is one aspect of group interaction I think is relevant at this point. I am referring to the work world or industry, which is beginning to recognize the importance of group energy and individual inspiration as a creative potential in the work place. In the past the rigid social structure of the industrial environment has tempted those who want to succeed—with the definition of success usually tied to the idea of making more money—to become slaves to their work. The term *workaholic* is sometimes used to describe those individuals obsessed by the need to work to near exhaustion with little regard for other aspects of life or pleasure.

Abraham Maslow (1964), the founder of humanistic psychology, showed how fulfillment at work or *self-actualization* as he called it, was based on personal satisfaction and growth in the workplace. Subjectively the individual enjoyed working, which provided satisfaction, joy, and happiness very different from the anxiety, stress, and exhaustion of the workaholic. Recently Garfield (1984) and others have shown how these *peak* experiences result from a different social atmosphere and organization in the workplace where frustrations, delays, and bureaucratic interference are minimized, resulting in new spontaneity and creativity for the worker. Conditions like these have characterized the therapeutic community (Jones, 1952) since its inception in 1947. Such a relatively democratic social system can apply equally to any hospital or factory environment (Argyris, 1970) or indeed to any purposive group activity.

Throughout this book are many references to, and descriptions of, therapeutic communities established in open social systems that form a model of an inspirational work environment peculiarly suitable for community projects for the aged. What started as an attempt to arouse the latent interest and activity among sociopaths and unemployed drifters in London 40 years ago has been adopted in part by mental health organizations and is now beginning to penetrate industry. As will be discussed later, open systems can be adopted by any social system, such as education, and can lead to an awareness of what lies beyond orthodox objective reasoning and learning in the intuitive, creative and spiritual realms beyond our ordinary consciousness.

In my experience this process of learning and growth requires a periodic exposure to a supportive and highly motivated peer group, with frequent discussions to look at and compare individual lifestyles and interpersonal differences of opinion. In time, sufficient trust may develop to risk exposing inner personal feelings to the group. We come to see ourselves through the eyes of the other group members. As individuals we discuss the unfamiliar or controversial and, even without realizing what is happening, we may incorporate new and congenial ideas and begin to think more creatively. In this way we widen our perspective on life's problems, and through social interaction we learn for ourselves and broaden our perspective as well as our understanding of life. Above all, we will probably sense the enormous potential energy and enthusiasm inherent in any motivated group that has a mission to pursue. Instead of passively accepting the conformist attitudes, we may begin to think for ourselves in both a personal and a group sense and begin to question the values and beliefs or our success-oriented Western society. Can we, as older people freed, at least in part, from a conformist culture make a significant contribution toward a world where wisdom and compassion transcend the materialistic and technological outlook threatening our very existence?

This highly subjective perspective summarizes my own use of the concept of the freedom of old age: to seek what is to me the meaning and purpose of life on earth. Everyone must explore options available for the optimal use of the freedom afforded by our later years, always bearing in mind that for some people less fortunate, mere survival may dominate their lives. Another important factor to consider in our later years, with its latent potential for change and growth, is the rapidly changing cultural scene in the west.

FUTURISM AND NEW AGE THINKING

The growing movement loosely termed *futurism* includes *New Age thinking* and aims at the integration of effort to humanize mankind's attitudes, values, and beliefs on a global scale. The various social organizations involved in achieving such goals as peace, human rights, and equal opportunity, have the potential to activate a growing awareness of our responsibilities not only to ourselves but to other nations and cultures.

Furturism is still a paradigm or a theoretical concept involving many things, including systems theory, ecology, economics, and morality, which are being slowly integrated into a plan for a healthier world climate. It represents a reexamination of the scientific reductivism of the past three hundred years, now being widened by the emergence of Eastern philosophies and an awareness among some physicists studying subatomic theory that the mysticism associated with this field bears a remarkable resemblance to the interest being generated by our gradual return to a spiritual awareness in the West.

Technology alone cannot solve the problems of world hunger, national debt, the drain on our energy resources—and above all the threat posed by the abuse of atomic energy in time of war. A new willingness to share our dwindling natural resources, to control overpopulation, and to teach our responsibilities to each other locally, nationally, and internationally is emerging. No one knows the answer to our world problems but, just as throughout history women have reflected the more humanistic values of mankind and opposed the abuse of power, so now it may be a time for the reemergence of the restraining influence of our elders to avoid catastrophe.

Is the aging population with its growing numbers playing its part to counter some of these excesses? This is a huge subject beyond my or anyone else's ability to conceptualize fully, but that cannot be used as an excuse for doing nothing. At the very least, we can ponder on our own contribution to a better world and bring our limited energy to bear on personal networks of acquaintances, and join other networks that are emerging on a national and international scale.

I know that, for myself, my basic belief in mankind and a lifetime spent in therapeutic communities has not dimmed my belief in the growth of a universal social responsibility. But the enormous resistance to change for the better in all sections of society has convinced me that good intentions, social engineering as in social systems for change, and religion are not enough. We all have ideals and an awareness of humane social values, but despite these factors we continue to live in and contribute to a world that belies this aspect of our better selves. We need a new beginning, and this is what the word *futurism* or the term *New Age thinking* reflects, however inadequately. This perspective gives my later life a sense of purpose and a freedom to pursue future goals that make this the most interesting period of my life.

The ultimate freedom means a chance to reexamine the concept of self and the way in which our environment and culture have shaped us. I must learn to listen to my inner self and question much of what I have come to take for granted. Ours is a youth culture with the mass media and advertising focused largely on the young. As an elderly person, I may feel a relative outsider in public places and may lack a peer group even in my social life. Competitive sport, which was loved in youth, may have lost some of its flavor. Only occasionally is there a thought-provoking program on TV or radio, and even then the nature of the medium makes interaction impossible. Where can I find fulfillment?

In response to such complex issues, there is, in addition to seeking a support group, a strong incentive to look inward and look for situations that still give inspiration, creative ideas, and energy. A feeling of inner joy, although elusive in a busy work world, can be found by anyone who seeks it, especially in a contemplative environment. Each individual must seek the environment personally conducive to inspiration—meditation, music, art, movement and so on (sometimes referred to in a generic sense as Dharma Art). It transcends what we know as the conscious mind limited by the objective reality of our five senses, time, and space. It leads us to a new awareness of the significance of intuition, synergism, synchronicity, dreams, and daydreams.

The word *synergism* relates to groups of people who meet voluntarily over time for a common purpose. Such groups usually discover that the group is more than the sum of its individual members, and a creative process is initiated that is not apparently related to any one of the individual group members.

Carl Jung (1951) introduced the word *synchronicity* to describe meaningful coincidences that no rational reasoning could explain. A person dreams of an airplane crash in which he is involved. Circumstances then conspire to make the person late to the airport and to miss a plane, which then crashes at takeoff. When one is alerted to the possibility of such inexplicable coincidences, they seem to occur with increasing frequency. This concept of synchronicity suggests an information network outside consciousness, which Jung called the *universal consciousness*, available to anyone who can break away from the strictures of our Western idea of an objective reality. He saw this phenomenon of synchronicity as a link with the Eastern philosophy related to a universal mind. To quote from Jean Bolen (1979), "Synchronicity is the Tao of psychology, relating the individual to the totality. If we personally realize that synchronicity is at work in our lives, we feel connected rather than isolated and estranged from others; we feel ourselves part of a divine, dynamic, interrelated universe" (p. 97).

We know that the world beyond reason exists, but it is not possible to prove this by reductive reasoning. This is the freedom to grow in the spiritual sense so often discouraged in a work-centered, money-oriented world.

My lifelong interest in support groups and communities epitomized by the creation of a therapeutic community four decades ago convinces me that we all need to be participants in a highly motivated support group, starting if possible in early childhood with groups of children and adults. This experience leads to a beginning awareness of deeper levels of consciousness than is usually found in ordinary life. For diverse reasons, such groups are rare in the adult world, being crowded out by other priorities, especially shortage of time. In later life, time is relatively freely available and a support group of some kind is for most of us a possibility, and in my experience is essential to a balanced life. It is the most practicable way to introduce the elderly and indeed all age groups to an awareness of a deeper level of consciousness and an awareness of the spiritual potential present in everyone.

These are some of the factors related to a feeling of freedom in later years associated with retirement. By contrast, in my work as a psychiatrist, I was impressed by the frequency of hypochondria in the elderly—as though the loneliness associated with children growing up and leaving home, the lack of excitement in the relationship with the spouse after many years of marriage, the growing social isolation and the relative loss of energy all sought solace in illness. This predicament led to the search for a doctor who cared (often fruitless) and frequently resulted in a heightened self-love. The "poor-me" syndrome (of fatigue, indigestion, insomnia, back pains, headaches, depression, etc.), had a disastrous effect on relationships with relatives and friends and blocked further personality growth for the individual.

As children we have all experienced a rich fantasy life, but our culture and education have impressed us with the importance of being realistic, and these early abstract trends have usually been stamped out, except perhaps in those who managed to find a career in the arts. But relics of this inner awareness are still manifest in adult life as dreams, intuition, or interest in the supernatural and the spiritual.

We all find it difficult to express in words feelings and ideas from this more abstract world. How can one express in words the subjective response to a sunset or a Beethoven symphony? Our language as we know it can to some extent describe the feelings associated with conscious emotions and sensory experiences such as pain, but it fails when we enter the spiritual or inner world beyond objective reality.

At a subjective level, I know that in the past decade I have largely departed from the rational reductive reasoning favored by the medical and scientific world to become increasingly interested in intuition and the spiritual side of life. I am not using the word *spiritual* in the usual Judeo-Christian religious sense associated with God. Now I *am* lost for words, even though I know that this experience is often as real as the reality that is available for what is characterized as objective proof. Luckily the world is changing and the growing interest in Eastern philosophies and in subatomic physics give support to the idea that much of life's experience cannot be explained rationally in words, and may never go beyond a subjective belief or paradigm.

These deeper levels of consciousness have not yet achieved credibility in many areas of our Western culture. In fact, the reductive scientific reasoning dating from the 17th century is still dominant in our educational system. For example, academic psychiatry and psychology, although they study the mind, do not usually introduce their students or their patients to spiritual ideas, and I was probably lucky to have an article published recently (Jones, 1986) bearing on this subject.

I'd like to think that the freedom from social and work pressures in old age and the approach of death are excellent reasons for us to contemplate and study these deeper levels of consciousness and their relationship with the next world—if any.

2

Education for Life
The Open System and Futurism

Few if any people are satisfied with the present state of the educational system, particularly if we believe it should be primarily a preparation for a fulfilling and useful life. The emphasis, however, is on acquiring knowledge in relation to ultimate employment—material success rather than maturity, ability to work efficiently rather than to think creatively—all of which contribute to the boredom so common in places of learning. The freedom to pursue study in an educational setting is becoming increasingly available to the aged, and, though it is often provided free, it is still the usual school and university curriculum. I have no illusions about the resistance to change in all forms of our bureaucratic practices, and education is no exception. There does, however, seem to be a growing awareness that, in general, students need more training in how to think for themselves as a first step to leading more creative lives.

Perhaps we who have lived long lives have a right to sit in judgment and say how education has or has not served our needs over the years. We suggest that this narrow view of education found in most schools of learning has little to do with the art of living and dying. It may be that this realization is more common with older people than with the younger age groups.

Young people often express high ideals—such as a life of public service—but when opportunity or encouragement are lacking they become disillusioned and, like so many other people, end up by serving self-interest in the form of money and power. Alternative approaches in preparation for a full and useful life would seem to call for a new outlook toward the whole purpose of school education as a preparation for life.

SOCRATES, SOCIAL INTERACTION, AND SOCIAL LEARNING

We all know that the quality of our relationships with other people is an essential ingredient in determining who we are and how we fit into our social environment. This being so, it is strange that relatively little attention is given to social relationships and individual responsibilities to self and others during our school years, particularly after elementary school.

Our preoccupation with material success in a competitive world may prevent the development of a natural interest in other people. As an example, failure to conform to the work or moral values of the school as reflected through the preferences or prejudices of the individual teacher usually leads to punishment of some sort. This means that although punishment may serve as a deterrent to the behavior in question, nothing is learned by either pupil or teacher. The meaning behind the failure of performance is not discussed, and an opportunity for growth in understanding for both parties is lost. There is relatively little interest or awareness of the determining factors that shape human behavior in the school environment. The teacher's role is determined at least in part by the curriculum laid down by the school authorities. The norms of schoolwork and behavior culminating in exams are rigid and amount to a process of conditioning for the pupil, supposedly in preparation for the employment world.

The factor of interest tends to be ignored—sacrificed to the needs of predetermined goals (exams) and stereotyped behavior. All this has been expressed in various ways on endless occasions, without significant change resulting. The inaction and refusal to change are all the more remarkable when put in a historical perspective.

Take for example Socrates, who lived in Athens over 2,000 years ago and who, according to Plato, believed self-knowledge to be the highest goal in life. In accordance with this goal he sought informal discussion often in the marketplace—but instead of answering questions he helped the individuals present to work out for themselves the answers to their own questions. Theodore Roszak (1978) has described Socrates as the midwife of learning, assuming as did Socrates that wisdom is present in everyone, and it only needs a helping hand to bring it forth. We do not know how far Socrates depended on what is today known as *group dynamics,* but his emphasis on the dictum of "know thyself" has a particular relevance at the present time. This is mainly because our attention is largely directed outward to the objective environment, and only recently have contemplation and meditation become more important in our Western culture. It is also important to note that Socrates talked about the soul in relation to one's inner self-knowledge.

PROCESS-GROUP INTERACTION AND PERSONAL GROWTH

Social interaction in a group of motivated people can have the same significance now as was the case 2,000 years ago. I use the term *social learning* to describe the *process* that inevitably accompanies such interaction. The various points of view expressed by individuals in relation to some topic of interest will not all be similar. The difference will be noted by each individual according to his own unique mind-set, and if accepted as something new, incorporated as part of his/her own makeup, or at least registered for future reference. This process of listening, interacting, and learning forms the essence of growth and change; how far this technique can be applied will depend on many variables, including the size and motivation of the group, the frequency of the meetings, the age, experience, and skill of the members, and their willingness to learn and grow. While such groups are largely associated with treatment in mental health facilities of all kinds, they are in my opinion even more relevant as growth or process groups in a school setting, or for seniors who choose to form support groups to counter loneliness and to contemplate collectively topics such as the meaning of life.

For instance, in the small university town where I live, the department of sociology sponsored the conference, Human Development in Later Life, in March, 1986, organized by Dr. Jeanette Auger, a gerontologist in the department. The conference was well attended, and in the later discussion we agreed to form a group to discuss problems of later life on a continuing basis. The response was immediate, and 11 people, mostly elderly, signed up, leaving their telephone numbers with us. Our first meeting occurred soon after this conference, and it was agreed that we would meet every two weeks in a room at the University of Acadia.

At our initial meeting each person gave a short statement about his present and past lives and indicated what he expected from the group. We had planned to have an interage mix, but not unexpectedly most people were over sixty and were predominantly female. I had hoped that we'd meet at least once a week, but everyone wanted a meeting every two weeks from 2:30 to 4:00 p.m. It was felt that the Canadian winter and difficulties in transportation would make more frequent meetings difficult. People were scattered over a 20-mile radius, but attendance has been fairly regular over the period of our existence, ranging from 6 to 10 people in the group.

At the very first meeting, the subject of death was introduced and to my surprise no one expressed any fear of this event. I wondered if this was partly due to a group member who worked as a nurse in a home for the elderly who said that although she had been frequently involved with terminal patients, it was a surprise to her that they never seemed to be afraid of dying. Maybe this firm statement from the authority of a nurse set the tone, and other members were not yet secure enough in the group to disagree. I said that until I was actually dying I couldn't tell how I'd react, but the subject fascinated me and we went on to discuss the writings of Drs. Elizabeth Kubler-Ross (1969) and Cicely Saunders (du Boulay, 1984).

At our second group, the subject of death and dying was again raised and now the group split into two parts over the idea of reincarnation, with the majority as disbelievers. Mother Theresa and her work in India with the dying seemed a safer topic to discuss than reincarnation. We also discussed the relative impotence of the church at times of need, especially for those lonely souls who avoided church and most religious and social activities. In this sense we saw ourselves as relatively privileged and as having the motivation, interest, and health to meet as we were doing—and not being reduced by circumstances to problems of mere survival.

These early groups were understandably about commonplace happenings, and the members seemed to be relieved to learn that they were not significantly different from their peers—and certainly not weird, as some tended to fear. For instance, one member said that she wondered if her growing forgetfulness was nature's way of softening our awareness of our diminished capacities, both physical and mental. This led to a lively discussion of the various ways people adjust to their limitations. A common one involves hearing. Why pretend to hear even when you don't? A supportive group allows people to practice requesting that others speak a bit louder, without appearing to be rude and at the same time helping others less ready to intervene. Other group members had various problems with eyesight, which sometimes added to their already slow movements due for example to stiff joints. We had all experienced falling down from not observing a step or from poor balance on slippery icy pavements. Everyone seemed to know how frequently the elderly suffered a fractured hip from relatively minor falls. I said that I'd decided to stop driving my car in our nearest city, Halifax, because I was aware of my slowed reactions when required to brake suddenly; and I felt that, despite the inconvenience and need to depend on another younger driver or public transport, it was a sensible precautionary measure. Everyone agreed that it was largely a decision we had to make for ourselves.

The group has solidified over time, and the level of trust has grown considerably. People have begun to talk about their inner selves and the difficulties in their lives, as well as about spiritual experiences. One woman looks after her ninety-three-year-old mother at home and shared, with obvious relief, how desperately trying this could be and how she appreciated a chance to share her feelings with others. She was determined to let her mother die at home even though "she's out of touch and can't communicate verbally." One group member described a vivid out-of-body experience (as though she was viewing from above what had until now been her own body) when, immediately following surgery, her heart and other vital signs stopped momentarily. Unlike most of these experiences described by Moody (1975), she wanted to come back to be with her young children. Another mother described how, many years ago, her son (then aged seven) saw God on top of a nearby house. He said nothing at the time, but some months later when asked if he believed in God, he replied, "Yes, of course," and added that he'd seen him clearly on the roof of a neighbor's house. The family was deeply impressed and made no attempt to undermine his belief, which they all seemed to envy.

At a more abstract level we discussed our social presence as we each saw this issue subjectively. Most people felt a growing loss of confidence in social gatherings, but one woman who'd been a director of nurse training at a university said she felt that they were lucky to have her there! And this attitude seemed to work. This positive note changed our focus to a more positive assessment of our place in society—for example, how children seemed to like the elderly who had more time to spend with them, which might mean listening more attentively to their stories than to their own parents.

All this may sound very ordinary. If so, then so much the better. We are not talking about group psychotherapy, as we are people who in no way regard ourselves as sick, but rather simply as people who are lonely or depressed by our circumstances, or uncertain in relation to problems which are inevitably a part of the process of aging. For us to have a peer group that is supportive and understanding is a great thing in itself. Everyone at one time or another testified to this factor.

We had 12 group meetings over a 6-month period; the advent of spring and summer was seen as an opportune time to have a break. We have a short summer in this part of the world, and the chance to enjoy the beautiful countryside in Atlantic Canada must not be missed. Everyone wants to reassemble in autumn because the group experience has become a significant aspect of our lives. One member suffered a minor stroke recently, but hopes to rejoin us later. I feel very much a member of this group, and being the oldest is, I think, an advantage that counters any tendency to see me as a leader with power. I try instead to be a *facilitator* and help the group to help themselves along Socratic lines. I see this as a growth group, but my psychodynamic experience in training and treatment groups has been useful. The group meets only twice a month, and this has almost certainly slowed the process of growth; and our relatively few meetings to date has meant that as yet no obvious interpersonal difficulties have emerged. There is a beginning tendency to confront me, which I welcome as a sign of confidence in my understanding and openness to criticism. A facilitator is to me a key role if process groups are to achieve their latent potential for growth or social learning and are to achieve their aim of helping the group members to think for themselves and not turn to the facilitator for the answers.

I realize how contradictory and controversial this may seem to many people. To be a facilitator is to assume a degree of responsibility for the social growth of the group, while at the same time denying the authority usually invested in a professional helper. You are helping the group members to use their latent potential and to work things out for themselves, acting like a "midwife of learning" by merely helping in the delivery of what is already there. I see no contradiction here, because from the start the group knew that I wanted to be seen as one of them and as an equal, while at the same time using my experience to help them to work things out for themselves. I am not the group leader and strenuously avoid attempts by the group to make me that. And a facilitator is *not* a teacher but is rather a group member whose experience is indicated by expressing possibilities—leaving the group members to follow through when a suggestion made by a facilitator seems to be appropriate. It is important to recall that this group grew out of a gerontology conference sponsored by the university and attended by the general public. The meeting place for our group was on the campus and so I was inevitably associated with the university. Until process groups became a familiar aspect of our ordinary lives at all ages (if that ever happens), groups will inevitably be under the umbrella of a social organization from which it derives its function and image, whether they be social activities, education, therapeutics, and so on. The role of a facilitator as outlined will inevitably reflect the encumbent's personality, but the overt aim is always to help the group members to realize their latent potential for social learning through their own efforts.

The process of growth releases energy, that mysterious attribute of that which is a significant factor in all creativity. Already after only 10 group meetings, we members are expressing our positive attitude to the group, which we feel releases energy and stimulates our thinking about the meaning of life.

ENERGY: THE INNER AND OUTER ATTRIBUTES OF MIND

In childhood, energy is expressed in play (outer) but also in fantasy (inner). The child's imagination allows the impossible to become possible (inner and outer) with no demand as yet to be rational or scientific. Parental influence or school, slowly or quickly, depending on circumstances, erode this freedom and attempt to replace it with reason ("reality"). This leads to a process of conditioning and conformity, the aim of which is to produce adults suited to an industrial society and, more recently, a communication society dominated by the mass media, by the computer, and by technology generally. The importance of acquiring facts and various kinds of knowledge is clearly essential if we are to survive in the modern world. It is the tendency to ignore our latent potential for growth in the areas of intuition, creativity, and our inner consciousness that has been sacrificed to our rational and scientific age. This is beginning to be realized by some parents and teachers, and I feel that in old age we might play an active part in rediscovering our neglected potential.

A child's failure to conform to this predetermined pattern is sometimes labeled by parents or school authorities as *deviancy*. Continued refusal to conform may provoke the disapproval of society and be attributed to sickness or sin, which in turn may lead to segregation or incarceration in an institution.

I see some parallels between the developmental hazards of early life and those accompanying retirement—with one major difference. Today society largely withholds interest and interference, hoping that the elderly will manage to cope somehow and not become a drain on the busy world of younger people. The *retiree* (horrible term) may react negatively with depression, anomie, or sickness—or by positively welcoming this freedom from interference. To me, this time in later life represents a second chance to grow—a chance that was denied in early childhood. The latent creativity present in everyone may be awakened even at this late stage. At last we are free to follow our inner drives through reading, social interaction, and listening—preferably including if possible a supportive discussion group. The latter is by far the most important development that I know of, if we are to become aware of the mystical and spiritual forces of which we are a part, transcending our rational selves.

If we consider the further development of social learning in a support group, the need for a training program will inevitably arise. Such training could include staff personnel from nearby homes for the aged as well as high school and university students interested in this field as a possible vocation. The interaged group already described has incorporated two students from our local university with such an interest. To enhance our skills as staff in training, we are starting a *process review* immediately after the group reassembles in the fall. I am deliberately blurring the boundaries between what we usually refer to as health and illness, and by implication avoiding diagnostic labeling as far as possible. Nevertheless, present-day society has to provide facilities for those aged persons who appear to be unable to look after themselves and who have no relatives or friends willing or able to undertake such home care. Many of these geriatric facilities are little more than survival centers without an atmosphere conducive to improvement and to a return to independent living. There are outstanding exceptions, but we are only beginning to realize the enormous potential of such residential facilities and the need to train people to achieve satisfaction in such a potentially creative vocation.

A review is an attempt to relive the process with the staff and students immediately following the community meeting, and to examine retrospectively the group process from beginning to end—a surprisingly difficult and demanding exercise. Did the group start on time? Who sat beside whom? Who spoke first? And so on. Verbal and nonverbal communication are recycled with a view to examining in a strict time sequence our differing reactions and frequently different perceptions of the same events we have all shared. Did we miss a cue, for example an interaction that lent itself to a superficial and misleading cover-up rather than helping the person in need to face the problem he is avoiding? Were we, as staff, defensive, blocking the group's criticism of our behavior or our lack of consistency in fulfilling an obligation to honor an agreement made in a previous group? And so on.

More subtle and demanding is our willingness to use the process review to listen to criticism from ourselves as staff, and to see this criticism as part of a process of social learning and not as a put-down or as reflecting interpersonal conflicts, rivalries, or lack of trust. The retrospective examination of individual performances in the group may be painful at times, but social learning is often a painful process. To discuss retrospectively what one did and why one did it in a group heightens everyone's sensitivity and skill. Not only can one focus on such things as the timing, sensitivity, and the aptness of one's inputs, but the complementarity of group members in reinforcing each other's inputs can be discussed. The further developments of the skills of the staff personnel and students as resource staff in connection with the various action groups designed to help the elderly to develop their latent potential will depend on many factors, in particular the wishes of the elder citizens themselves.

In a support group such as we are discussing, there is probably no inclination to professionalize the group, which is concerned with mental or psychological *health* not *illness*. Nevertheless a facilitator of some kind seems to be desirable to act as a catalyst and to help the group members to help themselves.

In my case I felt that what I had learned about group psychodynamics as a psychiatrist over a lifetime of group and community work in various settings was useful as long as I avoided the temptation to become a formal leader and impose my views on the group members. This concept of a facilitator is comparatively new in our time, but as already stated, it flourished in Greek times before Christianity was born. It may be premature at this stage to talk about a trainee group within the usual support group, but at some time in the future a process review after the group meeting may be useful to introduce students to an awareness of specific skills that enhance social learning in relation to themselves and the members of the interage group.

CULTURE AND THE CONCEPT OF HEALTH

There is no clear dividing line between what we call health and illness in the psychological sense, and we know that culture is a particularly important determinant. So the group we have been discussing may contain some marginally "ill" people who would probably be much worse if given a diagnostic label such as presenile dementia or neurosis by a well-meaning psychiatrist or mental health worker—especially if this image is reinforced by being referred to a doctor for treatment.

I am working toward the idea that our Western culture favors separating society into innumerable subgroups—like well or ill, young or old—which only isolate individuals unnecessarily from their natural peers, as in the case of illness or old age. To "become ill" is as significant a step culturally as it is medically, and may in time prove to be part of what Thomas

Szasz (1974) calls the "myth of mental illness." My concern is not with illness versus health, or even holistic health, but rather the retention of a spiritual awareness that is present in early childhood and then is suppressed by our culture and educational system but is never lost entirely. We have been talking about reviving this spiritual potential during the freedom of old age, but it would be better by far if it were allowed to survive and grow throughout life. As already pointed out, there have been periods in history during which spirituality was taken for granted and was a significant part of religion; and this circumstance persists to this day in many relatively underdeveloped cultures such as the Australian aborigines.

OPEN SYSTEMS, OPEN MINDS

The return of a more spiritual focus in our lives might well become possible if only we began to believe in the latent potential in every one of us to find this inner self. Let us start with the basic assumption that anyone who, when questioned, stops to think about the meaning of our lives on this earth will probably reply or imply that there must be more to life than the present struggle for money, power, and self-aggrandizement. I used to think this realization was more a characteristic of the old than of the young. However, I have recently had a pleasant surprise. Twelve student teachers at the local university asked me to participate in a group with them in order to learn more about themselves and their personalities in preparation for their future lives as schoolteachers. In this way, they hoped that they might understand better the problems of children in the classroom. I had met these students previously when invited by their professor to demonstrate open systems theory and method in his regular class. His approach to teaching was unusually liberal and the class was stimulated by experiencing a democratic system in a classroom setting along with a Socratic approach to social learning.

Despite the pressures of approaching exams, the volunteer group decided to meet three times a week during their lunch hour. So far, we have met on 16 occasions, with one marathon on a Sunday lasting 5 hours. From the first group meeting, they have shown a curiosity to explore beyond what is usually called the conscious mind and to share their inner feelings. This was helped because they knew each other fairly well, having been together as a class all year. It would take too long to describe the group process over the past two months of meetings, but I was amazed by the richness of their inner lives, which they had seldom if ever shared with other people. We heard of various forms of transcendental experiences—such as journeys into space, out-of-body experiences, automatic writing, hearing God's voice, thought transference—all accompanied by a surge of energy that might last for days. There were one or two students who seemed to be unable to get in touch with this spiritual part of themselves, but they still chose to remain with the group, for they too could see how these experiences in adult life reflected similar experiences in early childhood. In brief, these 12 students were all aware of the highly structured and conformist attitudes found in most educational systems ranging from elementary school to university. They hoped that in time they would be able to apply, at least in part, the social organization of an open system in their classrooms. They became aware, too, of the need to encourage the development of the fantasy life, spontaneity, intuition, and creativity found in the very young and counter the pressures to conform and to be rational with their classes when they are the teachers. They already knew that in future they would be largely dependent on the willingness to change on the part of the school authorities.

CONSCIOUSNESS AND SOCIAL CHANGE

The introduction of interactional group meetings, aided by an experienced facilitator outside the culture of the classroom, has the potential to transform human relationships and alter our social attitudes toward learning and personality growth. Moreover, if this growth process could be continued throughout the secondary school, university, and our other work and living situations up to and including old age, then we might work wonders for this troubled world of ours. In an age when despair and gloom are so commonplace, why not risk presenting a positive alternative! My own experience in schools (Jones & Stanford, 1973; Jones, 1974); in hospitals (Jones, 1982); in prisons (Jones, 1962, 1980); and in industry have convinced me that a democratic social system is an essential component of a harmonious and fulfilling work environment. The resistance to change in the traditional hierarchical social system makes it difficult if not impossible to achieve an open or democratic social system unless the sanctions from the top administration are favorable. Just as important is the development of support groups of the kind already described. These present an equally difficult proposition, again due to the resistance to openness so characteristic of our present-day competitive society.

The resistance to change in most social organizations, which I have fought against most of my professional life, only adds to the importance of groups for the elderly. Our experience of life and the frustrations caused by bureaucracy, along with other positive aspects of our freedom to contemplate and grow, may add to our incentive to play a significant role in changing our rigid authority structure.

The life cycle too plays a part. Children tend to see their grandparents as wise, the more so when they have more time to devote to their questions or to play with them than do their parents. The children will themselves probably become parents, and if their relationships with the two older generations have been positive and they have experienced open systems and supportive groups from childhood on, then a democratic environment may well be favored for the upbringing of their own children. In my experience, anyone who has participated in an open system will always seek to live in such an environment if possible for the rest of their lives.

The pessimist may well say that this is pie in the sky and life is not like that. Probably not, but there are many signs of change. My present experience with the two groups described is just one of endless examples of this cultural restlessness in the West. Another positive change in present-day youth is their remarkable maturity compared with anything I knew in my youth. This probably reflects the vastly improved communication networks demonstrated by various forms of global communication, computers, television, air transport, and the generally increased pace of living. It may be that the mass media largely reflects the negative aspects of life today—disenchanted youth brought up without love in broken homes, uninterested in a school system that ignores *their* areas of interest, dropping out from school and seeking the good life (which may be essentially materialistic—money, and the endless temptation to buy ever-more—exotic goods that are advertised wherever one looks). In an attempt to reach these goals without the necessary time-consuming training and being driven by impatience, they may turn to crime, reinforced by the knowledge that everywhere, even at the highest levels of our society, it is a common practice. This breakdown of morality, self-restraint, and discipline opens the way to an escape from the whole wicked world through artificial gratifications such as drink and drugs. In other words, what is sometimes called the consumer section in our society may well be the majority.

However, there is a counter-culture reflected by the conserver section, which even if represented by a minority of our youth, seems to be growing rapidly. They reflect the early maturity that I have just mentioned and aim to lead responsible lives, helping the less privileged individuals anywhere on earth, and are acutely conscious of our destructiveness not only toward mankind but also toward our natural resources and ecology generally. They tend to lead simple lives close to nature, and may live in communes or practice organic gardening, avoid excessive spending on luxuries, and wonder about the meaning of life. They tend to be seekers and, as my student group demonstrated, realize that there must be much more to life than money, power, and material success. The mass media tends to ignore this conserver section in our society, often preferring to highlight violence and crime as being more sensational. This reflects negatively on society rather than on the media, who must try to follow public demands even when they realize how detrimental their programs are by reinforcing negative values such as violence.

For the elderly who grew up in a different and less materialistic world, there may be a unique opportunity to look back on our material success and reflect on the seeming deterioration of our attitudes, values, and beliefs. If we can mobilize our resources to fight this excessive materialism, we may well regain some of our lost image of wisdom and leadership.

WESTERN MYSTICISM AND THE WESTERN CHURCH

We have already said that social learning is the result of conscious interaction in a group of motivated people with a common purpose, but what of a learning process that seems to operate outside full consciousness? We are not referring to the unconscious, which Sigmund Freud used to explain repressed ideas that manifest themselves in dreams and form the basis of psychoanalysis. Rather we are talking about the wisdom that has survived throughout history from earliest times and was a central part of our human understanding of the forces of nature and divine powers. To understand how we came to lose our awareness of the mystical or spiritual, it is necessary to consider the predominant role played by the Church in the evolution of our perception of body, mind, and spirit since early Christian times.

The known history of mystical thought dates from Judaism, centuries before Christianity was born. Although Christ's message of love was positive and full of hope, it was distorted by St. Augustine in the 4th century into a preoccupation with sin and damnation. Driven underground because it was a sin to question the teachings of the Church, mysticism somehow survived through the Middle Ages. Survival was due to Sufi tradition linked to Islam and to the various culture carriers, such as the creative architects and builders of the great Gothic cathedrals of Europe beginning in the 12th century, who later became known as the wandering Freemasons (Harman & Rheingold, 1984). Despite the attempts by the Catholic Church to persecute those who promoted mysticism or strayed from the Church's dogma regarding the dangers of deviancy and sin, the concepts of creativity and mysticism were never lost. From the 17th century, knowledge was no longer limited to the Church, and creative thinkers like Francis Bacon in England and Rene Descartes in France contributed to the new growth of science and education. For the next 300 years, science was preoccupied with reductive reasoning, claiming that ultimately everything could be understood by a process of logical reasoning and subjected to proof. It is only since the beginning of this century that this form of objective absolutism has begun to be questioned.

Many factors have contributed to this partial break away from objective proof. Among the most important are scientists (especially physicists) who no longer feel limited by the rigid parameters of our five senses, time, and space. Following Albert Einstein's discoveries regarding relativity, the splitting of the atom and subatomic theory, quantum mechanics, and many other factors, scientific reductivism has had to be modified. Indirect studies of invisible particles, energy, light, and so forth, have had to be considered seriously, and proof gave way to probabilities in these areas; some of these findings have been termed mystical by the scientists themselves (Capra, 1982; Krishnamurti & Bohm, 1985).

In a somewhat similar way, helped by a surge of interest in Eastern philosophies, the rigidities of orthodox religions are being questioned by free thinkers like Matthew Fox (1983) and Bede Griffiths (1982), both priests of the Roman Catholic Church. They see common denominators in all religions, both Eastern and Western. Included are such studies as philosophy, anthropology, mythology, psychology, and aboriginal cultures that survive in may parts of the world where the shaman's art is still practiced (Harner, 1986).

In recent decades the idea of holism has spread rapidly, implying that everything in this world relates to everything else. In religion this can be taken to mean that God is part of every individual; in medicine that not only are all parts of the body interrelated and interdependent, but this applies to the environment too—and so on in every aspect of life.

The implications of this holistic philosophy are tremendous and affect all our lives. Old people can look back and wonder about the limitations of the rat race of employment, which often precluded the time and energy for self-examination, let alone serious social interaction, reading, or study. In a sense we are lucky to be old and free at this time in history. The world is changing at an ever-increasing rate, mainly as a result of the new technologies. But the main actors in this drama, with some brilliant exceptions, are too busy in their respective fields to pay much attention to holism. Atomic science applied to the atom bomb is a glaring and terrifying example of this blinkered vision.

Where do we elders fit into all this? For those of us who are able to enjoy our new freedoms, I can think of no better objective than to contemplate the innumerable facets of a holistic philosophy. We are what we do, and in the process we affect everyone and everything in our environment. Such an attitude usually leads to a greater feeling of social responsibility, which in turn leads to various forms of social interaction. The energy we derive from such interaction often produces community action groups like the peace movement, environmentalists, natural food enthusiasts, discussion groups, open education and so on.

HOLISM VERSUS THE CLOSED SYSTEM

Holism is meaningless as an isolated phenomenon and to be of any effect it must be part of a system that theoretically affects everything else in the environment. But we all know of systems that fail to thrive or that end in chaos. This calls for another dimension of holism in the form of systems theory.

Systems theory defies definition and is more a concept or a paradigm that evolves where groups of people are assembled for a common purpose. Our usual models for such systems are in such areas as industry, politics, health and welfare, where the power and authority rest in one or more top people. Such systems, often called closed systems, are hierarchical and are the antithesis of holism. What the world seems to lack are open or democratic systems where everyone belongs and has a say in the social organization and decision-making process of the total organization. In holistic terms, such an organization has a positive impact on the environment through workers and their families being relatively free from the stresses of a closed system. They feel insulated from sudden changes in the workplace (unexpected layoffs, etc.) and help in making suggestions at times of crisis as well as being able to enjoy all the benefits of an open communication network.

We must also strive to get beyond our preoccupation with objective phenomena, a reflection of the scientific world, and seek understanding of our inner selves or the soul. Modern psychology (Deikman, 1982), religion (Fox, 1983), and philosophy (Needleman, 1980) recognize this. Although we know the meaning of virtue, we seem to lack the will to live according to the dictates of truth and goodness. Nor do we seem strongly motivated to look inwards and ask, "Who am I?"—being largely preoccupied with the material world and our values of power, money, and self-advancement. Unfortunately, more technology such as computer science, while leading to more and more data collection, does not necessarily mean more wisdom (Roszak, 1987).

Only in recent times have we begun to think of ourselves as a mix of body, mind, and spirit. We are beginning to realize that technology alone is not enough to save the world from destruction. We have to find out more about our inner selves, implying a latent creativity outside our consciousness, before we can hope to bring about any lasting change in a global sense; otherwise history will continue to demonstrate that we are incapable of learning the folly of repetitive wars and other aspects of human self-seeking. The terms *inner consciousness, mysticism,* and *spirituality* are necessarily vague, being outside objective study and outside of the vocabulary to describe them. However, intuition is a familiar concept to most people. We tend to think of intuition as some mysterious or supernatural happening, but it is also conceivable that as we learn more about the brain there may be a neurochemical explanation of intuition. It is possible also that the presently limited view of an objective reality may be transcended by the coming together of millions of neurone batteries in a holistic matrix outside our formal consciousness, in what we might call a "flash of insight." Such a phenomenon is often associated with genius.

The mystique of genius may also be an example of this gray area between an holistic brain/mind and spirituality. Many creative artists like Mozart, Kipling, and Wagner have stated clearly that inspiration usually comes in a twilight state between sleeping and waking, in dreams, or in trancelike states, suggesting that there are states outside ordinary consciousness that are unfortunately relatively inaccessible to most of us (Harman & Rheingold, 1984). However, everyone probably has experiences in adult life that defy logical explanation, and which remain private for fear of ridicule. In this context the well-known phenomena surrounding the fantasy life of children are strangely overlooked in our whole educational system, presumably because of our preoccupation with facts and logical reasoning. Artists are the lucky ones who may escape from this tyranny.

However, thanks to many factors—including the recent interest in Eastern philosophies; the emergence of New Age physics and subatomic theory (Zukav, 1979; Capra, 1975, 1982); the development of a creation spirituality (Fox, 1983); the work of mythologists such as Joseph Campbell (1972) and Jungian psychoanalysts such as Jean Bolen (1979); and the study of native cultures in many parts of the world where the shaman's tradition survives (Harner, 1986)—a new holistic approach to philosophy (Needleman, 1980) has conspired to shake the complacency or our rational view of reality.

In this chapter we have followed a rather tortuous path into the largely unknown world of mysticism. Our purpose is not to criticize education as the pursuit of knowledge, the basis of our Western civilization. Rather, we attempt to expose our lack of interest in education in the spectrum leading from the quality of human relationships through discussion groups to synergism, synchronicity, intuition, holism, systems theory, spirituality, and beyond objective reality to a new reality outside our formal consciousness.

This is admittedly highly speculative, but there is much evidence to suggest that a transformation of our culture from a preoccupation with conformity to a more spiritual reality is occurring even now (Ferguson, 1980; Capra, 1982; Krishnamurti & Bohm, 1985). If this belief in the emergence of a more spiritual/mystical global culture than we now know is fulfilled, we will be getting much closer to a deeper meaning of life for everyone on this earth.

Anticipating the future—far from being a game—may in the opinion of many thinking people be our last chance for global survival. Going on this assumption, I believe that education must play a central role in contributing to this change in values from a preoccupation with self-interest and rationalism to a global spiritual perspective.

I believe that such an outlook has a special significance for the elderly who over a lifetime have seen the follies of materialism and a success philosophy, and in anticipating the end of life are moved to ask themselves, "Who am I?" and "What is the meaning of life?"

3

Communities As Support Systems

Since my school days in Edinburgh, Scotland, I have always been a team player (cricket, rugby, etc.) and "playing the game" was a cherished ideal for me and most of my peers. Unfortunately, as you grow older there are progressively fewer "players" and, anyway, playing the game seems hopelessly dated and I have felt progressively isolated.

For the major part of my working life I have been preoccupied with the integration of effort in connection with the treatment of various kinds of social casualties with stigmatizing labels—from *schizophrenia* to *sociopath*. My training as a medical doctor had a profound influence on my view of treatment, which seemed to mean doing something to the submissive needy person without invoking that person's participation and help. At first I felt trapped by the orthodoxy of medicine and took my Hippocratic Oath seriously, based on the ideals and principles of the ancient Greek physician Hippocrates. As time passed, disillusionment set in and I saw how even the concept of confidentiality was open to abuse, as it catered to the power and prestige of the doctor to an inordinate degree and implied a lack of accountability between the doctor, patient, and the family. In recent years, family therapy and other more democratic practices such as the growth of patient rights (Ziegenfuss, 1983) have eroded this doctor power. In a more democratic society the patient, the family, and the doctor could come together routinely in open discussion and social learning could result for all participants—listening, interacting, and learning.

COMMUNITY IN EXTREMIS

Fortune favored me in my search for a more congenial environment in which to put into practice some of these goals and achieve a more informal relationship with both staff and those patients who came to us for help.

At the beginning of World War II, I was thirty-three years old and had achieved respectability as a psychiatrist, being the assistant to the Professor of Post Graduate Psychiatry in London. I was assigned to be in charge of a clinical research unit of 100 beds to study an obscure heart condition associated with young soldier recruits suddenly thrown into the stresses accompanying training for combat duties. We had a constant turnover of 100 soldier clients, a professional staff of doctors, nurses, and research personnel, and the unique freedom from bureaucratic control that wartime circumstances occasionally allowed. Situated on the outskirts of London, this clinical research unit experienced the intimacy that the German bombing of London engendered in the population, and which resulted in a remarkable feeling of togetherness among most of the seven million inhabitants.

Symptomatic of this closeness was the behavior shown by everyone in our hospital on the occasion of incendiary bombs dropped on us by the Luftwaffe on a winter's night. Half of our accommodation was quickly on fire and, to my surprise and delight, our move to the previously prepared funk holes dug on the hospital grounds went as smoothly as a holiday picnic outing!

Immediately following this temporary relocation of our patients in the underground shelters, the research personnel were free to rescue some of the more precious equipment and record files from the burning buildings, praying inwardly that the German airmen had gone home without waiting to deliver their load of high explosives.

When relatively small groups of people are thrown together by the circumstances of war and are living in close proximity, they sometimes experience an illusion of invulnerability that transcends the fear of personal injury. The number of people seems to be important; thus, in the Royal Navy the destroyer crews fared much better than the larger, more anonymous battleship crews. Our unit of some 150 personnel came into this favored category. Not surprisingly, this opportunity to enhance the significance of proximity, close social contact, a common purpose, and mutual trust slowly changed the original hospital hierarchy to an increasingly democratic one (Jones, 1952).

Since that time 45 years ago, my interest in supportive groups and communities has grown steadily, and my first book, Social Psychiatry: A Study of Therapeutic Communities, written in collaboration with six of my colleagues, was published in 1952. Five other publications have appeared, the last in 1982. The original hospital setting has been widened to include prisons, schools, industry and other social organizations.

GROUP SUPPORT FOR THE AGING PROCESS

The same general principles apply whatever the setting, but we will focus mainly on the elderly population and begin with the aging process itself. Each age carries an implicit label, not unlike the labels attach to disease. Between the ages of forty and fifty is the beginning of middle age for most people. Certain stereotypes are common, such as youth is over, so I'd better watch my weight, or abandon strenuous exercise, or become more health conscious. For women, pregnancy is discouraged, the youthful face, figure and vitality are on the wane; for singles, marriage is improbable and, as with men, the lifespan begins to seem very limited. At fifty, all these factors are reinforced, as physical evidences of aging seem evident to all, while for women the menopause may have a significance often far beyond the biological facts. Health hazards to life, such as coronary disease and cancer, may assume enormous, even hypochondriacal, importance. At sixty, there is all this and more, with the specter of retirement to further demoralize many people; while in the seventies, horizons narrow further and Old Man Time with his scythe is beginning to cut down all too many of our peer group. At eighty, most of our former friends are gone and we wonder who's next. I've purposively painted a gloomy picture of growing isolation to highlight the significance of support systems aimed at minimizing the plight of otherwise solitary and vulnerable elderly people, particularly the poor and the physically or mentally handicapped.

In Western countries, the culture has until recently favored the young at the expense of the old. In most Eastern countries such as China, the wisdom and judgment of the elderly, especially men, is still highly regarded—which is not to deny that many elderly are stupid and many young people are wise. The important thing is that they are accorded a high status in their culture and so are not as prone to be devalued as in our Western society. This Western prejudice is understandable in part, when a progressive neurological condition like Alzheimer's disease is present, but not when the label old implies a mythical senile degenerative disease of the nervous system. There is mounting evidence that mental powers need not decline with age (Novak, 1985; *Brain/Mind Bulletin*, 1986). To quote from the latter, "When children become more thoughtful and less impulsive we say they are maturing; when elderly people spend more time in thought, we call them senile. They may show more wisdom and insight because of (slower thinking)." This particular issue of the *Bulletin* cites several current research projects based on the premise that psychological development may peak in old age.

Another important factor contributing to the disadvantage of being old is that throughout history the extended family (or tribe) has been an extension of the individual self. This meant that even in death or calamity a part of the individual lived on through the survivors. In a somewhat similar way the survival as a tribe was dependent on a bountiful nature, which nevertheless was inscrutable, unpredictable, and immensely powerful. So the idea of a deity emerged, to become a religion in later times. However, in more recent history the power of the church has been eroded to be partly replaced some 300 years ago by scientific "truth." Since the 1960s there has been a slow decline in respect for tradition and institutional values such as respect for the law, politics, and education. Respect for the aged has also been subject to this decline, and we have tended to become increasingly isolated and vulnerable. It is probable that no one can maintain a balanced perspective in isolation, and we believe that a peer group with frequent social interaction is necessary if the process of growth and maturation is to continue into old age.

To be deprived of the stimulation of social intercourse is a minor form of sensory deprivation. When sensory impressions from the world around us are deliberately cut off, we lose our self-awareness and may disintegrate into a state of mind akin to "madness" in extreme cases. Joseph Campbell (1972), a well-known mythologist, has pointed out that from a mythological point of view, the thought disorder that we label as schizophrenia is identical with the thought disorder found in Carl Jung's concept of archetypes, with the mystical state common to shamans in various parts of the world, and finally with the states of mind associated with drugs such as LSD. In brief, there seems to be a common or universal pool of thought patterns outside our formal consciousness that is inaccessible to the Western mind except in circumstances of a mystical nature such as those outlined in the last chapter, or by a discipline of the mind as achieved by yoga or a sudden transformational experience. This may sound like meaningless abstraction to many people, but such observations seem to reinforce the possibility that the concept of an individual self may be a fiction, and that we are indeed tiny particles of a universal whole, a concept familiar both to some theologians (Fox, 1983) and to subatomic physicists (Zukov, 1979) alike.

GROUP ENERGY

There are many social organizations involved with care for the elderly, but we are primarily concerned with social interaction that brings about growth within a social system for change. The concept of social learning was elaborated in Chapter 2, with particular reference to schools. The same general principles apply to any group that includes the elderly.

We have stressed the importance of group interaction among motivated people as a prelude to social change. In retrospect I now realize how the energy liberated in such a setting had a peculiar fascination for me and sharpened my awareness so that at such times I seemed to think and interact far beyond my usual level. Nor did the number of people present seem to be particularly important. It was a common (daily) practice to interact with our total population of approximately 100 patients and staff at the original therapeutic community near London where I worked for 12 years between 1947 and 1959. The more usual groups of 8 to 10 people were also held daily and, although predominantly psychoanalytical in nature, they too shared in this periodic feeling of enhanced performance and energy increase, even though the focus was on individual problems in a group setting.

I have already mentioned my preoccupation with team sports in my school days, which went far beyond the interest and energy directed toward schoolwork. It is only now that I see the value of exploring the possible complementarity between these two extremes; losing oneself in a team identity in competitive sport and disciplining one's mind in individual study—the enhanced energy and ability in the former and (when interest is absent for the student), the unproductive drain in energy in the latter. By contrast, study in a group matrix, especially if a facilitator or tutor is present, can evoke the same energy that characterizes a team in sport. The application of this principle has already been noted in various settings, as described in Chapter 2 on education.

A residential community is the optimal setting for this enhanced energy and performance, and seems to apply whether we are talking about a therapeutic community in a hospital or a residential conference. Esalen Institute in California is an example of the latter. It is mainly for studies in New Age topics for up to one hundred people, living together for days, or a long-term stay as a student. There are literally hundreds of these residential communities for learning, among the earliest being the time-honored monasteries in many parts of the world, the ashrams of India and elsewhere, the modern survival courses sponsored by various educational organizations, and so on. Many of these communities offer training in the eastern philosophies and other New Age subjects not usually taught in our schools.

QUALITY OF RELATIONSHIPS

Social interaction in group and community meetings raises the question of the quality of the relationship we have with ourselves. Do we understand ourselves? Can we metaphorically speaking, stand back and watch our behavior as though looking at another person? Arthur Deikman calls this the *observing self* (1982), which is outside consciousness and does not belong to the domains of thinking, feeling, or action. He states, "If the mystics are correct, through properly guided self-observation we can begin our escape from the circle of self-centeredness to a new realm of freedom and a new source of self-knowledge."

We believe that everyone has an awareness that there are forces vastly greater than our individual selves, of which we have only indirect knowledge and which we designate as mystical, spiritual, or the soul. My own experience with group interaction has helped me to recognize synergism, synchronicity, intuition, creativity, and the mystical as described in relation to social learning in Chapter 2. Most people can recall incidents in ordinary life when they experienced a flash of insight or an awareness beyond the reach of their conscious mind. We all are familiar with accounts of prophetic dreams, thought transference (usually from a close friend), strong premonitions of positive outcomes or disaster, a voice from a departed friend or relative, or even detailed instructions from a hidden source.

A Support System Outside Consciousness

One of the most extraordinary accounts of a parapsychological event is *A Course in Miracles* published by the Foundation for Inner Peace (1981). This account, believed to be transmitted by Jesus through an agnostic professor of psychology at a university in New York, boggles the mind. A woman professor working in collaboration with the head of her university department found herself trapped by an incomprehensible inner compulsion to record almost daily the messages transmitted by a force outside herself. These she shared regularly with her senior university colleague. She needed constant reassurance that she was not going mad, and her more objective partner stressed that the material she was transcribing was not only sane, but was beyond reproach on ethical grounds, being compatible with a message from Heaven. In brief, this transcribed material accumulated over a period of eight years required no editing and ultimately reached 622 pages of typescript! As already mentioned, the scribe was agnostic, but by good fortune she was able to take shorthand with unusual speed. To quote from a shortened version of *A Course in Miracles* (1981), "the Course is a reteaching of eternal truths, presented as a self-study course for personal transformation. It is a spiritual teaching, not a religion. It uses Christian terminology but is ecumenical in nature." In essence the message is of unconditional love, and that sin, fear, and guilt are the direct result of lack of love.

Whatever one may think about abstract "miraculous" experiences such as the one described, it does pass one essential criterion of validity—it has proved to be an invaluable guide to many practicing psychotherapists. Judith Skutch, who actively promoted the publication of *A Course in Miracles* (1981) is herself a psychotherapist who makes extensive use of this material, as do a great number of other therapists. One of the best known is a psychiatrist, Gerald Jampolsky (1985) whose books have a wide circulation. He started the Center for Attitudinal Healing in California in 1975, as well as two organizations associated with children. Children for Peace has as its goal children talking to children about peace on a global scale. The other organization uses children who are often terminally ill to counsel other equally tragic victims regarding the process of dying and the value of group support at a spiritual level.

At the other end of the age spectrum, Gay Luce has pioneered a nonresidential day center for elderly people in the United States. This was started in 1974 with a group of 12 volunteers between the ages of sixty-three and seventy-seven in a large house in Berkeley, California. Her staff was unpaid volunteer professionals from the Bay Area. The daily program was flexible and varied, reflecting the individual skills of the staff. The elderly were free to go to whatever activity appealed to them at any one time. A major focus was on meditation and various forms of movement, biofeedback, and relaxation. The program helped the group members to learn from each other by sharing experiences, and so forth, but not to discuss or attempt to solve personal problems. Gay Luce reports on the rapid growth of a climate of intense commitment. "The experience was synergistic," and by 1978 the organization, which was known as SAGE, was known nationally, helped by a documentary film, and 24 similar projects had been started in other U.S. cities. A large group involving everyone was held one day a week, usually lasting three or four hours but sometimes lasting all day. There is not sufficient information to know exactly the form and purpose of these groups, which were probably essentially administrative, because problem solving at a personal level was discouraged. What is important is that the dedication to the group became intense, and everyone felt an atmosphere of excitement and mutual discovery. Something was happening to these relatively isolated elderly people to awaken their dormant self-confidence and creativity. Gay Luce describes how she herself was positively affected by this experience. She has training as a transpersonal psychologist and teaches at San Francisco State College; she has become well known for her advanced ideas and holistic health philosophy. In her book *Your Second Life* (1979) she talks about old age being a time of truth and can be a major transition. "The more we can talk about this transition, the more we can accept the greater reality that is our lives" It seems to me that, like our group, she was focusing on the group's latent potential for personality growth rather than on psychotherapy and problem solving.

To return to our ongoing interage group focusing on the problems of aging, we must admit to being a long way from the residential communities we have touched on, but nevertheless the same group energy is easily recognized. Richard Moss (1981), talking about groups in general, states, "As this process is going in many people at once, the sum of such actions potentiates the process in each, and perhaps gives rise to sufficient energy to allow penetration into new levels of reality" (p. 112). This is similar to the concept of synergism where the group is more than the sum of its individual parts.

SOCIAL AND FAMILY SUPPORT SYSTEMS

Assuming that people need people is a comfortable generalization but does not seem to apply to everyone. Some families remain as a relatively closed system, less dependent on others for a support system than is commonly supposed.

When I was a child five years old, my father died at a comparatively early age and my mother decided to leave South Africa for the sake of the education of her three children. She had lived most of her life in the United Kingdom, but her mother was now dead and her father was a successful businessman in the U.S.A. To live in his world would have been entirely practicable, but she herself had had an extensive education in the U.K. and preferred to return to a system and a country that she knew and loved so well. Having no income or capital of her own, she had to rely on erratic financial support from her father and decided to live in Edinburgh in Scotland, where education was good and inexpensive. She knew no one there and literally lived for her three young children. She died when I was in my thirties. Her unselfishness had resulted in her three children all having a good education. I had chosen a career in psychiatry. My elder brother was a Queen's Counsel at the Scottish bar, and my sister was teaching elocution at the university. Her selflessness was undoubtedly an inspiration for me, but I'll never know the full extent of her sacrifice because she never mentioned such matters. On the other hand, my sister became a widow after only four years of harmonious marriage and was childless. She died recently at the age of eighty-three, and in her later years we became very close to each other. It was only then that I realized the full extent of her loneliness in Edinburgh. My brother is also dead, but although he was apparently happily married, the couple had no children, and I always felt that his wife was compared unfavorably with his mother whom he adored.

I mention my intimate family because my perception of supportive groups is inevitably colored by what I know best. Always more sociable than my siblings and inheriting something of my mother's passion to help others, I gravitated to medicine and then to social psychiatry with an emphasis on group work and residential communities. This lifestyle has always afforded me an unusual feeling of togetherness in both work and leisure. Nowadays I feel a delightful intimacy with my three young adult daughters, who were all conceived in my first marriage and have enjoyed a very full, creative, and happy marriage with my third wife over the past 11 years. So in brief, social relationships have always been a constant source of joy and inspiration to me in both leisure and work.

Nevertheless, it is only now, with the steady demise of my peer group, the limitations of my physical mobility, my diminishing capacity to keep up with my much younger wife, and the loss of much of my group and community work, that I am experiencing something of the meaning of loneliness. My response to this feeling is to follow a developing trend that started about a decade ago in my active group work and almost automatically leads to the realm beyond formal consciousness. This contemplative solution feels right for me, but I recognize the danger of prescribing this course for others, especially as I am probably happier now at the age of eighty than at any previous period of my life, and I am insulated from the stresses of survival both economically and in terms of health, which is still sufficiently good to allow me to enjoy people when I'm lucky enough to find kindred spirits.

I doubt if the relative immobility of the elderly is as great a handicap as it might appear to younger age groups. As an example, sex has a differing significance over the period of a long life, particularly when one allows for changing cultural patterns. I had mixed feelings about the sexual freedoms enjoyed by youth in the 1960s and 1970s—part envy and part distaste. Without really resolving these uncertainties because I was already too old to participate actively or unselfconsciously, it was still possible to enjoy my work and domestic life without indulging in the new sexual freedoms. More pressing cultural problems have emerged in the 1980s, particularly in connection with the changing role of women and the so-called feminist movement. As a young man in Scotland, respect for women was a dominant cultural pattern and was expressed overtly in good manners, courtesy, dressing for dances and other formal occasions, and so on. My first sexual penetration was at the age of twenty-eight when I was a research fellow at an American university. The action was initiated primarily by an uncommonly attractive American female undergraduate who programmed the seduction—admittedly to my extreme delight. I rather think that my first wife had more to do with the planning for our three girls than I had. I was in no way reluctant, but the initiative seemed to be hers. Suddenly, during the past decade, my feeling of equality and complementarity with women is shattered by the emergent feminists. As a result I find my social confidence eroded on social occasions, when I'm automatically labeled by word or implication as another macho male by female friends or casual contacts. My training and practice as a psychiatrist have insulated me from prejudice regarding homosexuality within either sex, and I still see it as a liberating trend. Nevertheless, I come from a generation where the husband was characteristically the wage earner, the wife ran the house, and extramarital affairs, if any, were hushed up. I remember no tendency for men to be more unfaithful than women, but there was a code of secrecy subscribed to by both sexes. Also, in a very real and helpful way, the lack of adequate or safe contraceptives made conservative practices a virtue. Fear of contracting AIDS is having a similar effect at the present time. We had none of the computerlike detail of today, exposing all the nuances of intimate sexuality, with the confident arrogance of this technological age—as though statistical facts spoke the truth. In a similar way, the female form is portrayed by the media so explicitly that the intimacy of the bedroom may become something of an anticlimax.

As with most things, nature has a tendency to balance or compensate for the ravages of time, and through both lack of opportunity and lack of desire, most of us are content to be relatively inactive sexually in old age. For me, the fantasies and memories of the past have an enhanced charm, stripped of the realities and stresses of the original event. The energy associated with sexual attraction tends to be diversified to make study and contemplation even more attractive and rewarding as a substitute.

INNER ENERGY

It is as though contact with one's inner self may be followed by a feeling of joyousness and energy, as though one is momentarily freed from the braking force of reality. On the negative side, a deep disappointment or loss may open the floodgates of despair, and momentarily everything associated with self is filled with nothingness. Either way, the experience may last from minutes to months, or lead to a transformation of one's self-image that persists for a lifetime. To the Buddhists the positive realization of freedom implies freedom from self, or selflessness. It is believed that the practice of meditation and the adoption of a guru or leader can, over time, bring this about at least in part. On a more generic scale, energy, whether positive or negative, involves the whole person and his environment symbolized by heaven or hell. In either case, it is no longer "me," but rather, "I'm an insignificant part of an ongoing process beyond my capacity to conceptualize." We seem to be at a crossroads in respect to reality. Our whole culture and education seek objective proof through our senses and the power of reason. The new reality bypasses objective proof and opens the way to an intuitive awareness of something vastly greater than self. By escaping from the bonds of a materialist, techno-logical, scientific world, we seem to discover the secret of the universe, which includes everything known and unknown to man. To the Christian this means symbolically the Holy Trinity —Father, Son, and the Holy Spirit. Again we are intuitively aware of the energy and joyousness emanating from such an awareness. From the conversion of Saul to become St. Paul, to Martin Luther King's "dream." What a contrast to our ordinary lives when even the privileged university student tends to be drained of energy by the combination of an overloaded sched-ule, prescribed reading, and exams, leaving no time for contem-plation and self-awareness.

Most people have an awareness of the concept of body, mind and spirit. We put enormous emphasis on body and mind, but for reasons that are elusive, we neglect the spirit. However, in my experience, this state of affairs is more apparent than real. As an example, I have already discussed in Chapter 2 the partic-ipation in two regularly scheduled groups, each comprising approximately ten people. One, an interage group, is predomi-nantly made up of people over sixty; the other group comprises students studying to become school teachers. Both groups are volunteers and both are process groups without any specific goals other than open communication regarding problems of living. Not unexpectedly, the elderly group is preoccupied with the past and the meaning of life and death; while the students, to my amazement, are primarily concerned with *IT*, the term they coined at our initial meeting to express the idea that there is much more to life than our material world is willing to recog-nize. The elderly group seems to be made up of seekers who look beyond the frontier of death epitomized by the woman in her late sixties who, during surgery, stopped breathing and later described her out-of-body experience. She looked down on her own body and floated toward a radiance that filled her with joy. But on being returned to her body by medical resuscitation she was pleased, for her children needed her. The student group likewise seeks understanding of the spiritual side of life. They knew each other well, having been together for almost a year and with one or two exceptions seemed to be willing to share their inner thoughts. One young woman described a particular tree in the country to which she felt bonded and where she could find inspiration by just relaxing there. Another said she had decided to leave teaching as a profession and to start a home for the aged, which they would be free to run largely for themselves. A young man had felt deeply troubled a few days previously and, unable to sleep, he had lit a candle and sat looking at the flame. He developed a feeling of motion and was being transported to some unknown destination and experienced intense joy. After what seemed to be only minutes, he looked at his watch and realized to his amazement that more than an hour had passed. In both groups the idea of the spirit or spirituality seems to transcend our usual concept of a conscious mind. It implies a letting go of our usual rational thinking and opening our minds to ideas not usually available to our conscious minds, and to the conflicting forces that contribute to the ever-present anxiety we experience even though we may deny this. At the other end of the feeling spectrum from anxiety is joyfulness and energy, which breaks through periodically in a process group, but is also a familiar occurrence in our interpersonal relationships.

JOYFULNESS AS A SOURCE OF ENERGY

What is it that constitutes this state of mind in some people and not in others? We can all bring to mind such people. They seem to generate energy in us and others around them. Even here, where I live in a small university town of 3,000 inhabitants, I immediately think of a dental receptionist, a salesperson in a health food store, and a professor at the local university —two women and one man. The two women I barely know, but seek to contact whenever possible, often for no apparent reason, which may puzzle them, but never seems to change their attitude toward me. Maybe I reflect back to them the resonance they give me, so that they see themselves through me as a mirror. I never cease to hope that circumstances will bring us together somehow, but maybe I hesitate to break the spell for fear of losing the magic they hold for me. The third person, the professor, is entirely different. We met by chance three years ago when I found him to be an insecure, anxious, and somewhat pedantic person who overcompensated for his negative self-image by talking too much, mostly about his world. Somewhat reluctantly I responded to his overtures, and as a result I found that his inner need for understanding seemed to arouse an inner response in me that I did not really understand. I learned that he was deeply religious and liked dogs to the extent that he was sought out to be a judge in various dog shows. As I shared neither of these attributes, I continued to be circumspect and somewhat skeptical. Then I saw him with some of his students toward whom he radiated vitality and for whom he really seemed to care. This, and because he became known to me as a risk taker, dramatically changed my image of him. If necessary, he was prepared to fight any abuse of authority, especially if it concerned his students, and even jeopardize his own job security in the process. Resonating to these characteristics, I was now included in his category of people who preferred principle to conformity, and I now saw the joyfulness he showed in the presence of certain people whom he trusted and who needed his help. He was overtly a change agent who broke away from the conformity characterizing his university department, and as a result he was labeled as unreliable and at times irresponsible.

In the first two instances described above, I'm content to enjoy the experience without seeking to understand it. With the professor, a serious attempt at understanding him led to the discovery that, in certain circumstances, we transcend the judgmental limitations of reason, and find the excitement and energy that we accept joyously, without feeling a need to analyze the situation. In retrospect, this form of letting go is something beyond our usual practice of alert awareness, accompanied by a need to understand and control in order to circumvent fear and anxiety: the what-if phenomenon. Trust is part of this state of mind, but we seem to be entering a condition beyond what is commonly understood as the conscious mind.

Is joyfulness part of the process of letting go in relation to an objective criterion of what is rational, forgetting the ever-present dangers of deviancy our culture conditions us to expect? It is certainly different from the happiness we experience on winning a lottery or defeating an opponent, where the reasons appear to be self-evident. Is it a submission to fate, whatever that means, or is it an awareness of something far beyond our finite selves? This state of mind seems to have come easily to our early civilizations where people accepted their helplessness and turned to higher forces to protect them. So nature and a deity were accepted without question, and body, mind, and spirit of today was more like spirit, body, and mind of that time. Our belief in God has slowly been transposed and replaced by a belief in man's resourcefulness and technology to solve our problems. Luckily, the spirituality inherent in mankind, while dimmed by a shallow religiosity in recent centuries, was never lost, and seems to be enjoying a resurgence today helped by our beginning global consciousness and awareness of Eastern religions.

At a personal level, I had a spiritual experience three years ago that made a profound impression on me. I was invited to Rome to help in training some personnel associated with drug-treatment programs. The group comprised 25 staff from drug units all over Italy, as well as two parents of drug addicts. The aim was to demonstrate an open system by involving everyone present in group interaction for five consecutive days. A Roman Catholic nun acted as my simultaneous translator. We decided to meet as one group for six hours a day, with a break for lunch and two intermediate coffee breaks. The meetings followed lines that one expects with a motivated group—interaction, emotional disturbances of various kinds, listening, learning, and a growing group identification and trust level. On the second to the last day, one of the two parents, a former Alitalia pilot with 30 years of service to his credit, broke down and wept when talking about the other parent in the group who had lost his son from an overdose. He felt deeply for the other parent, having himself lost a daughter to drugs. The group had given him a new feeling of hope. He went on to say that he would not want this person as his parent but nevertheless had loving feelings toward him. The group talked about the power of love and how the group was helping the members to re-evaluate their own attitudes and beliefs. The group seemed to close in upon itself, and several of us had synergistic feelings of another presence added to our group.

On the next and final day, the group climate was disruptive and negative. It was apparent that there was a strong resistance to return to the previous day's feeling of an abstract presence in the group. However, in the final hour the pilot chose to return to his reminiscences. He described how a former air pilot colleague who had soon to retire on account of age had felt himself a failure because he had never qualified to fly the newer jet planes. He had tried unsuccessfully to help this man. This precipitated a sudden loss of interest in flying himself, and he left his job as a pilot, never to return. This happened many years ago, but the incident was still vivid in his mind. The group was obviously moved by his distress and empathy, and suddenly a silence descended on us and lasted several minutes. This time the feeling of a presence was so strong that everyone seemed to be overawed into silence. The nun who was sitting beside me and who had acted as simultaneous translator from English to Italian, said quietly, "A state of grace." The group melted away without a word. None of the usual thank you's or expressions of gratitude for a useful, if stressful, workshop, and so on. A departure from the traditional that spoke volumes. I walked into the garden and, standing alone, wept tears of joy —a feeling that returns whenever I recall this incident.

Retrospectively, everyone seemed to agree that we had participated in a mystical experience of a unique kind. This incident followed an unusually satisfactory five-day group-process experience for me, and the others with whom I interacted before their departure felt the same (everyone was in residence at the Conference Center). This center was in the shadow of the Pope's summer residence at Castel Gandolfo. It is situated in a beautiful setting and is beside the largest drug-treatment center in Italy. This center is visited occasionally by the Pope, and the Holy Father lends his support to the whole drug-treatment program in Italy.

For me, although I am not a Roman Catholic, the social climate had a religious and, at times, a spiritual flavor; and in our spontaneous group discussions in the evening we often shared our mystical experiences. I found myself enjoying the freedom to discuss concepts such as Carl Jung's synchronicity and how Rupert Sheldrake's (1981) ideas on morphic resonance had been helped during a prolonged stay at Father Bede Griffith's ashram in southern India—also, the New Age physics epitomized by a book on quantum theory, *The Dancing Wu Li Masters*, (Zukav, 1979). The other group members gave fascinating accounts of their spiritual experiences in their lives as priests, drug addicts in remission, and so on.

In brief, I feel that my innate scientific skepticism had been replaced by a readiness to be open to intuitive and paranormal experiences in a semireligious setting. I have described my social-group experiences over a lifetime, from team sports as a schoolboy to my present circumstances as a resident in a small university town in Nova Scotia. In retrospect, I can see how an evolutionary process has emerged as an unbroken thread, always seeking to uncover the latent potential inherent in any group of like-minded people. Even in London during our early days as a therapeutic community, we were sensing the power of an open system before we had evolved a conceptual framework to depict the phenomenon, and before systems theory enjoyed the prominence it has today. As with most people of my advanced age, the success once enjoyed as a pioneer in social psychiatry and as a change agent has faded for me and in the minds of everyone even distantly involved, but I still derive energy from the often joyful memories of those days.

The glamour of consulting at universities such as Harvard, Stanford, Toronto, or London has been replaced by occasional visits to places of healing such as drug and alcohol units, or to places of education where open systems are seen as relevant. However, circumstances of health and limited energy have now largely restricted my active interests to beyond human consciousness—to the third area of the triad of body, mind, and spirit. To have gravitated to a small university town can be passed off as chance or luck, but I prefer to see it as the final stage of a consistent life process as a seeker—as though I am now willing to submit to forces beyond my ken. In all this, my wife has been my major confidante and guide. As an example, we arrived here five years ago to share a workshop on open systems with the Atlantic Provinces Psychiatric Association. After four days of seminars it suddenly occurred to us that we'd like to live here and leave Phoenix, Arizona, our domicile for the previous five years. So we bought our present home before returning to Arizona to wind up our affairs there. I like the idea of *submission* in this context. It was an unpremeditated decision, more intuitive than reasoned, and arrived at in an unfamiliar environment during a four-day visit.

My wife spends her time in her chosen field of wood sculpture. I have had a wonderful time relating to the university, literally wandering about the campus and meeting people as circumstances permit. My original sponsors in Nova Scotian psychiatry had no direct contact with Acadia University, which has no medical school, so the initiative to live here was no more rational than that it felt right for us both.

4

Death, Dying, and the Aftermath

At first sight, to say anything about dying appears absurd, or at least presumptive. And yet at a subjective level, I feel I'm already in transition. The relative freedom from commitment that many, if not most elderly experience would seem to demand a considerable concentration on the subject of death. To me, this long-term perspective offers an exciting adventure into the unknown. The outlook from where I sit in my office is inspiring. The many moods of nature come to have the familiarity of intimates. As dusk falls and the objective reality of the tree-covered slope dims, a new inner awareness emerges. There is a confusion of fleeting images that defy description, like dreams in the waking state freed from the censorship of the mind. My identity surrenders itself to the forces of nature; when the skies are clear the sunset bathes the scene with a joyous flood of gold, and I am part of the mystery of life. This is part of the ultimate freedom referred to in the title of this book. No matter how much suffering, hopelessness, and frustration have been part of an active working life, the freedom of later life can open the door to the beauty of the world all around us. But we need to take time to leave our urgent problems even momentarily and focus on the meaning of life and our inevitable transition to death.

I hate to see the aging process in my own body. Is this vanity, or simply a failed attempt to stay young? To say, "I am not my body" seems a little wiser, as it still leaves room for remaining young in mind and spirit and keeps the door open for a life after death. To make matters worse (or better?), my medical training explains why I have to get up at night to "we-we" and why, apart from this inconvenience, the actual time spent sleeping becomes shorter. This trend is compensated by an often embarrassing new tendency to fall asleep when interest flags—a message seldom lost on whoever is speaking at the time and who rightly sees this as a message that he or she is boring to me! Nor need I categorize the other signs and symptoms associated with the entire length of the alimentary tract, the reproductive tract, and so on. It's a bit like an old car when the exact site and cause of the rattles and unfamiliar noises tend to become unimportant. The funny thing is that writing seems to be less inhibited than in the past, and I enjoy the feeling of confidence and creativity even while knowing that this may be an illusion—at such times my physical failings seem rather irrelevant.

I like this concept of relativity applied to bodily symptoms. Even in childhood I learned the value of indulging my aches and pains to invoke sympathy from my kindly mother, or even missing school for health reasons without sharing the real reason with my parent. This body/mind duality persists throughout life—without implying any hint of faking, we all know how interest and positive attitudes have an inverse relationship with pain. This may reach what to an observer approaches heroic proportions, as in the following example, where severe postoperative pain was almost forgotten in an emotionally charged dialogue.

Is there a parallel between the process of aging and readiness for death itself? Many people seem to demonstrate this by dying as they lived. For example, some months ago one of my closest friends, a man of great compassion and integrity, died in South Africa. His daughter wrote, "He didn't seem to be afraid to die." Talking to this daughter a few hours before the end, he had said:

"I've got a question for you, Doris. Should time go slower or should it go faster?"

"Oh, Jesus, Dad, that's difficult. Is this another riddle?"

"Yes, it is."

"Must I answer it for you, or for me?"

"For me—what do you think?"

"Okay. I think you want it to go slower because it's only two weeks since you knew you were going to die, and that's a short time to do the thinking you want to do. On the other hand, you know you are not thinking so clearly now, and that is concerning and irritating you. To lose the power of rational thought is the one thing that is fundamentally unacceptable to you." [He was a surgeon.] "So on balance I should think you want it to go faster."

"Quite right. If time was three times faster now, it wouldn't be fast enough."

He died within hours, apparently content that he was no longer a burden to his much-loved family.

The most beautiful and thought-provoking account of death I know of concerns the last days of Gregory Bateson as recounted by his daughter, Catherine Bateson, the only child of Gregory and Margaret Mead, his first wife (M. C. Bateson, 1980). The account opens with the following statement:

Just as the intimacies of childbirth and early mothering have gradually been restored, first with natural childbirth and rooming in and most recently with childbirth in the home, so there is a growing effort to meet death more intimately and simply. The logical end of this development is that people die at home or in an environment as close to home as possible. The depressions which used to afflict mothers after childbirth are probably related to interruptions in the early intimacy between mother and child which plays a biological role in the establishment of parental love and care. Similarly, the shadows of guilt and anger which so often complicate grief may also be related to interruptions in the process of caring, and they may be lightened by the experience of tending someone we love with our own hands, so that much that seems externally repellent and painful is transmuted by tenderness. (p. 4.)

What makes this account unique is the clarity and honesty of the details of the process of death written with both compassion and objectivity by Gregory Bateson's anthropologist daughter.

Most people, if given a choice, would probably prefer to die at home surrounded by those closest to them. The environment of a hospital is peculiarly unsuitable. The hospital personnel, conditioned to the idea of implementing a cure, or at least being able to provide help of some kind, seem to foster an atmosphere of denial in the face of terminal illness, and they avoid expressing their inner feelings even among themselves or with the patient and his family.

PIONEER WORK ON THE FRONTIERS OF DYING

It was this anomalous state of affairs that motivated Dame Cicely Saunders to change matters by developing an optimal environment in which to die. But it was a long struggle, over a period of almost 20 years, and it is beautifully described by her biographer, Shirley du Boulay (1984). Despite having trained as a nurse and as a medical social worker, Saunders realized that it was only by becoming a doctor that she would have the authority to make changes in conditions for the dying possible. So in 1957 at the age of thirty-three she started her medical training and was a distinguished student. After qualifying as a doctor, she obtained a research grant and she chose to work with the dying in St. Joseph's Hospital in Hackney, London.

The first and most fundamental change she introduced— the regular giving of drugs—came straight from another hospital, St. Luke's. She was allowed to try four patients on this system and it was so successful that she was encouraged to use it more widely. She started by prescribing the drugs the nuns were already using, mostly Omnopon, but gradually introduced a morphine mixture and heroin. The medical profession has always been nervous about giving these drugs frequently, fearful of the drugs' addictive properties, or that the patient would become tolerant of their effects and the drugs would cease to be effective. Cicely's detailed studies, admired by Dr. Winner, the Principal Medical Officer in the Ministry of Health responsible for London, proved empirically that this need not be so. Writing in the *Nursing Mirror,* Cicely says:

> Constant pain needs constant control, and that means that drugs should be given regularly so that the pain is kept in remission all the time. If a patient has his own dose of analgesics given to him as a routine he is not then nearly so dependent, either upon the staff or upon the drugs. If every time you have a pain you have to ask for something to relieve it, you are reminded each time of your dependence upon the drug itself, but if your medicine arrives routinely before the pain takes hold, this does not happen. This is important, for a patient's independence must be maintained in every possible way. We find that under this system we are hardly troubled at all with either tolerance or addiction, and that when we have correctly assessed the patient's need for dosage, I am convinced that it is far more often because the patient's pain is getting worse as his lesion extends than because he has become tolerant to the effect of the analgesic. (p. 70)

And in *Current Medicine and Drugs,* she writes even more confidently:

> It is our experience that if pain is kept permanently in remission tolerance is remarkably slow in developing and may never appear. We have patients on the same dosage for months and even years, and many who have had drugs on request before they come to us are able to have less analgesic in the twenty-hours once control has been established. (p 71)

Anyone reading the biography of Cicely Saunders will be impressed by the extraordinary quality of her dedication to the dying. At the age of thirty she experienced her first love, with a man whom she was nursing, and the account of their relationship during the two weeks before he died is a revelation and an inspiration. It was this intimate knowledge of the suffering and unnecessary pain in the terminally ill that inspired her to devote her life to creating an environment catering specifically to the needs of the dying.

While working as a doctor at St. Joseph's, she was also busy planning the ultimate goal of a hospice designed exclusively to meet the needs of the dying. Her purpose was strengthened by a second love affair with a dying patient, which lasted only three weeks. Her first love had been 12 years previously, but now her resolve was strengthened further by the depth of her emotions for this man and his family. Her cause was gaining public support with an increasing momentum, and her contacts included many famous and influential people. Finally, in July, 1967, her dream was realized and the first patient was admitted to the new facility, which had been named St. Christopher's Hospice.

There are now scores of hospices for the dying in the U.K., and a survey done in the U. S. in 1984 by the National Hospice Organization showed that nationwide a total of 935 hospices were serving 19,000 terminally ill patients and their families. Of these, approximately 15 percent receive inpatient care in hospice facilities, the rest receiving hospice services while living at home.

In 1980, Saunders married a Polish artist whose painting had attracted her 17 years previously—particularly a blue crucifixion in oil. On the basis of this picture, the first she'd ever purchased, an intense relationship grew up with the artist, culminating in her marriage at the age of sixty-two. My wife and I spent some time with them in Rome when we were attending a conference on drug addiction. We went together to an audience with the Pope. It was touching to see the Polish artist, armed with one of his paintings of the Virgin Mary, give his present to the Holy Father, which seemed to inspire the Pope even more than Cicely Saunders herself! An interesting reflection on the power of culture in relation to social values.

THE FRONTIERS BEYOND

The other outstanding pioneer in the field of dying is Dr. Elizabeth Kubler-Ross, whose book *On Death and Dying* published in 1969 has been widely acclaimed. It was she who drew attention to the phenomenon of the out-of-body experience often found in people who have been near death (on the operating table, in accidents, etc.). On recovering, these people have frequently described how they appeared to themselves to have left their bodies and had watched the activity to revive them from a few feet above their bodies. Raymond Moody (1975) has endorsed Kubler-Ross's findings and he has collected over one hundred examples of this near-death out-of-body experience. The value of these experiences is to draw attention to what may be a look at life after death. Moody gives a composite picture of the cases he studied in detail, which describes the main features of this phenomenon:

A man is dying and, as he reaches the point of greatest physical distress, he hears himself pronounced dead by his doctor. He begins to hear an uncomfortable noise, a loud ringing or buzzing, and at the same time feels himself moving very rapidly through a long dark tunnel. After this, he suddenly finds himself outside of his own physical body, but still in the immediate physical environment, and he sees his own body from a distance, as though he is a spectator. He watches the resuscitation attempt from this unusual vantage point and is in a state of emotional upheaval.

After a while, he collects himself and becomes more accustomed to his odd condition. He notices that he still has a "body," but one of a very different nature and with very different powers from the physical body he has left behind. Soon other things begin to happen. Others come to meet and help him. He glimpses the spirits of relatives and friends who have already died, and a loving, warm spirit of a kind he has never encountered before—a being of light—appears before him. This being asks him a question, nonverbally, to make him evaluate his life and helps him along by showing him a panoramic, instantaneous playback of the major events of his life. At some point he finds himself approaching some sort of barrier or border, apparently representing the limit between earthly life and the next life. Yet, he finds that he must go back to the earth, that the time for his death has not yet come. At this point he resists, for by now he is taken up with his experiences in the afterlife and does not want to return. He is overwhelmed by intense feelings of joy, love and peace. Despite his attitude though, he somehow reunites with his physical body and lives.

Later he tries to tell others, but he has trouble doing so. In the first place, he can find no human words adequate to describe these unearthly episodes. He also finds that others scoff, so he stops telling other people. Still, the experience affects his life profoundly, especially his views about death and its relationship to life. (Moody, 1975, pp. 24-25)

While Kubler-Ross is by her own standards a scientific researcher, she is also an action-orientated individual. Her work on near-death out-of-body experiences leads her to explore personally the world of spiritualism and mediums. This has taken enormous courage and has cost her dearly. Her family and friends have deserted her, and despite her enormous contribution to society in her research work and clinical practices with the process of dying, her credibility has been severely shaken.

By contrast, Moody's studies have been largely theoretical, based on careful interviews to gather information retrospectively from the subjects of near-death experiences. A Ph.D. in philosophy, and an M.D., Moody sought confirmation of his near-death findings by studying other resource material such as the Bible, the writings of Plato, and the Tibetan Book of the Dead. The parallel findings from these sources and his own studies make fascinating reading.

One of the many important findings from these studies is the comparative frequency of out-of-body experiences. It seems that people are afraid to talk because they might be seen as nutty even by friends and family, so this information tends to be hidden. This applies to most mystical experiences, and one can admire the way Kubler-Ross has ignored public opinion and has talked openly about her experiences with spirit guides. However, it seems inevitable that the cultural climate is changing, as evidenced by the spate of publications related to this field.

Shirley MacLaine's film and book *Out on a Limb*, (1983), probably caused a quantum leap in public acceptance of such abstract ideas, and her value and prestige as an entertainer may have saved her from much of the pain and ridicule that others, like Kubler-Ross, have suffered—after all, doctors are expected to be conservative and predictable!

I have thought a good deal about my own attitude toward death and dying. This fluctuates from day to day according to circumstance. If I have read some inspiring book like Raymond Moody's *Life After Life* (1975) then I can see how out-of-body experiences in people who have been resuscitated after being pronounced dead tell remarkably convincing and consistent stories of their joy at seeing the brilliantly illuminated presence of God; moreover their experience seems to obliterate any doubt about ultimate survival. Kubler-Ross has observed similar experiences among her dying cases and describes their reluctance, when pronounced dead, to return to this earth. Or I may derive comfort from listening to a devout Roman Catholic who has an unquestioning belief in an afterlife and who surrenders willingly to the last sacrament administered by a priest.

OUR RESPONSIBILITY TOWARD DEATH
AND THE AFTERMATH

In the final analysis I know that it is my responsibility to be as ready as possible for my demise. The more I read, contemplate, and discuss, the more my attitude tends to harden and a greater consistency emerge.

At the scientific or rational level I know that New Age physicists with their researches into subatomic theory have been awed by the mystical qualities of matter, which when reduced to the smallest possible particles is without substance. They are forced to the conclusion that many phenomena may never be proved or understood, but nevertheless are part of our reality. I have come to accept that our ideas and even our language have been based almost entirely on objective observations, while subjective awareness, imagination, and intuition so typical of early childhood are largely ignored in our adult lives and discounted by our educational system.

At a personal level I know that my sister, who died recently at the age of 83, was laughing happily minutes before her death and had never doubted the existence of life after death. Like my mother, she was a warm-hearted and generous person who asked very little of life but gave freely. We probably all know people to whom death seemed to be an episode without the terrifying reality that our Western culture has tended to produce. Many people even tend to deny awareness of the slow process of disintegration that is an inevitable preliminary to the final "illness" of old age. For me, perhaps due to my medical training, it is an interesting process of change, and this applies to the whole person of body, mind, and spirit. At an abstract or subjective level I notice many changing attitudes and perceptions. People *look* different and communicate more through their behavior than with words. I *feel* their presence less through sensate awareness than through their effects on my energy. Some people almost invariably make me feel more alive, and every aspect of my positive awareness is heightened, while negative factors like worry, gloom, and even pain are bypassed. Recently I went with my wife to listen to the singing of Rita MacNeil to a capacity audience of 1,500 people in the Acadia University Hall. Some people might describe her as fat and jolly, but it was her warmth and love that transcended the negative and made one feel glad to be alive. At the present state of our knowledge, we can only guess at the meaning of interpersonal transmission of energy and use words like *inspiration* or *resonance* to describe what happens. At a spiritual level it implies uplifting fantasies or universal feelings beyond time and space, as with those fantasies of celestial music or angels singing—or whatever a person's cultural heritage identifies as being akin to this state of mind. It is increasingly evident that all cultures, religions, and philosophies contain common elements that transcend time and feel like *the truth*. This applies to the process of dying and the afterlife. In early times, this was sometimes seen as part of a natural cycle—like the seasons —and had the quality of fulfillment.

If we choose to think in a historical perspective, it is worth remembering that in the Middle East royal tombs over 3,000 years old have been found to contain multiple graves wherein a king and his queen were buried together with their retinues: "Both the animals and the human beings had been buried in the monstrous grave alive; the court ladies lying peacefully in rows in court regalia" p. 64 (Campbell, 1972). This was done in preparation for rebirth through death.

There is also the paramount difference between the philosophies and religions of East and West, where the Western preoccupation with the individual ego and a lifetime search for self-fulfillment is in sharp contrast to Eastern selflessness and repudiation of the ego.

It seems to me that our Western Christianity and its message of an afterlife is based largely on faith and belief in Christ's teachings about a Heavenly Father and the resurrection. Moreover, during the past 300 years, scientific reductivism and rational thinking have tended to obscure a belief in Christianity as lacking in solid proof. This materialistic outlook repudiates the idea of an afterlife, again due to lack of proof.

THE HOLOGRAPHIC PARADIGM

The recent past, since the 1970s, has seen a remarkable coming together of both science and religion and a beginning recognition that each requires the other if we are to gain further understanding of the spiritual or transcendental world beyond what we ordinarily term the conscious mind. In this context, Karl Pribram, a neuroscientist, and David Bohm, a physicist, have between them proposed theories that call for a new perception of reality. They propose that what we ordinarily describe as reality is based on the evidence of our senses, time, and space, and may be an illusion. By combining the evidence derived from holography with theoretical physics, which has demonstrated that at subatomic levels the familiar process of scientific reductivism cannot be used, a paradigm shift may be emerging that anticipates a new or primary reality. This new reality belongs to a domain beyond time and space (or ordinary reality) and may help to explain transcendental experiences such as precognition, psychokinesis, time distortion, rapid learning, and some "miraculous" forms of healing. In brief, Pribram postulates that if the brain is a hologram and that ordinary sensory reality is a construct of the brain's mathematics drawn from a still-hypothetical real reality, then it is from this latter reality that we derive our transcendental experiences and our awareness of the infinite. This whole field is immensely complex and hypothetical, but is described in *The Holographic Paradigm*, edited by Ken Wilber (1982). The concept of the hologram may require an understanding of physics to understand fully. However, I think it is important to introduce this concept of a new paradigm that may open up the possibility of explaining the new reality and the possibility of a better understanding of transcendental thought.

We have already mentioned on several occasions how a counter-culture is emerging that repudiates this limited scientific or rational argument and favors a much wider or holistic perspective that combines the philosophies and perspectives of East and West, rational and speculative, objective and subjective, right and left brain, and so on. The idea of spirituality takes us beyond the boundaries of rational thinking, which has dominated Western thinking and education since the 17th century. It opens up a world as yet largely unexplored, where the idea of a person as an individual may be a myth, and where we are all perhaps part of a universal whole. To me this is a comforting concept linking mind, body, and spirit. Death is then terminal only for our physical body, and the soul or spirit lives on in some as-yet-unknown way.

I have put forward a point of view that demands a considerable amount of study if the holographic paradigm or the concepts implicit in holism or futurism are to be understood. But at an intuitive level, the mystical is familiar to us all, especially during childhood and, in adult life, in dreams and daydreams. I suggest that old age is the ideal time in life to explore this latent potential in preparation for the end of our life on earth.

5

Spirituality

Spirituality is a state of being rather than a mind concept, and so it is hard to put into words. This difficulty was lessened for me by a recent set of circumstances that must seem familiar to many people of my age. When should one surrender the common self-image built up over a lifetime and submit to the reality of a circumscribed and physically limited new lifestyle? This happened to me over a two-month period while I was working on this final chapter, and has, I think, helped me to write it.

Of the Need to Surrender

Since leaving full-time work and before my recent infirmity, I have been privileged to travel overseas at least twice every year in connection with teaching assignments in the areas of democratic social systems and group work. Such invitations have the appeal of working for a week or two with motivated people who are predisposed to social learning and change. For the last two years my health has deteriorated in response to the stresses of this overseas travel, and more particularly the emotional involvement in numerous teaching seminars. This stress was especially true on return visits, where the process of growth was evident and the expectations of me as a facilitator were greater. I had already resigned myself to eliminate cherished visits to Rome to help in the field of drug addiction, but I had thought that at least one more visit to the U.K. was feasible.

The goal was a community project that has many unique features and a spiritual environment beyond anything I'd ever experienced. This House of Affirmation is a residential community for Roman Catholic priests and nuns who need time out to contemplate and reconsider their lifestyles in a supportive environment. Society may call them ill, but they feel this is an empty phrase or at least too narrow a concept to satisfy them if they enter treatment. Perhaps it might be likened more to an Eastern ashram modified to suit our culture. With a staff of seven and twice as many residents, an intimate atmosphere is easily obtained and there are moments—especially at midday mass—when the atmosphere can only be described as mystical.

The Sister in charge is a remarkable woman who radiates integrity and trust, and at the daily community meetings with all twenty personnel present, the overall level of trust is an invitation to soul searching. Not only was I in constant contact with these people at mealtimes, informal groups in the evening and so on, but there were daily training seminars with the staff where, inevitably, interpersonal problems surfaced. I mention all this to indicate my justification in returning yet again to an environment that epitomized the optimal setting for social interaction, learning, and change in a group of 20 highly motivated individuals, but which left me emotionally and physically drained, even if happy. Anginal attacks came with alarming frequency and indicated a heart muscle demanding rest or else!

Back in Nova Scotia the symptoms of congestive heart

failure spoke eloquently of the need to surrender to a simple and restricted pattern of life possibly limited to my home environment. The view from my office window is if anything more beautiful than ever and the birds more precious. Yes, I want to live a little longer, with a wife whom I love, and continue my search for the Holy Grail and a better understanding of the transcendental. It is in this frame of mind that I look forward to writing down my thoughts on spirituality.

CONTEMPLATION OF THE WHOLE

In the days before leaving routine work, I paid little attention to the spiritual dimension of life. I had the usual exposure to Scottish Presbyterianism and went to church in Edinburgh most Sundays with my mother, who was a firm believer in God and the hereafter. I was attracted by the Rev. George MacLeod, our minister at St. Cuthbert's whom I knew superficially. He later left this wealthy parish to work among the poor and the underprivileged on the River Clyde near Glasgow, and also set about rebuilding the abbey in Iona where St. Columba had landed from Ireland and brought Christianity to Scotland.

The previous chapters in this book have traced the tenuous course followed by my colleagues and I in progressing from group and community work to a growing awareness of the intangible forces in the environment, like synergism (the group is more than the sum of its individual parts) and synchronicity (coincidences not apparently the result of cause and effect). I'd like to think that our early community work in the 1940s and 1950s reflected and even anticipated some of the present-day holistic tendencies to see the interrelationship and interdependence of all things pertaining to life on earth. I do know that the momentum of my 40 years of practice in an open system caused me to recognize ever-widening parameters in human relationships and the importance of spiritual factors in human understanding and behavior. Like many people, I see a growing integration of body, mind and spirit and a unifying trend in religion and philosophy.

As an example of this common trend, Father Bede Griffiths, a Benedictine monk, has lived in an ashram in Southern India for the past 30 years. He has made a special study of Hinduism as well as the other Oriental religions and believes that although they represent a very different approach to God compared to the Semitic religions, Judaism, Islam, and Christianity, they are nevertheless complementary (Griffiths, 1982, 1983). He describes his ashram as a place of utter simplicity with numerous huts in a cocoanut grove and a communal eating place for up to seventy people. People of all persuasions are welcome and stay for varying periods of time. They can live in isolation in a hut or interact with Bede Griffiths or other people at will. It is a place of peace and prayer close to nature where you try to find yourself by submission to a higher power.

This man has influenced me more than anyone in my search for "truth" even though I have never met him and my health negates a stay in his ashram. A friend who is a psychiatrist at the House of Affirmation in England has spent three months at his ashram and reflects the influence of Father Bede Griffiths in an environment that has much in common with an ashram.

AT HOME IN THE ASHRAM

Like many people, I need living reminders of what I believe to be the good life and in this context try to build my own "ashram" in the environment of my study—the only possible answer that I know to my dilemma of immobility. Here is my place of peace where I can contemplate while viewing the wonder of nature outside. In winter the stark trees on the hillside will on occasion assume a beautiful form usually associated with the Virgin Mary, who for obscure reasons beyond my comprehension has for a long time had some particular fascination for me. The form is static but beautiful and reminds me strongly of the similar vision I experienced at St. Peter's in Rome. I am surprised to find how content I am to spend most of my time alone in my office, made necessary by my failing health. My desk faces a huge picture window looking out on an unspoiled tree-covered hillside that has become a friend whose mood changes with the light, the wind, and the animal life.

Old age reminiscing in our culture tends to be equated with a somewhat boring interruption of everyday topical conversation or gossip but reminiscing in one's private space may be seen as linked to contemplation. If, for example, I've listened to an audiotape spoken by Bede Griffiths and feel his presence nearby, and am watching nature's changing scene outside my window, I feel like surrendering my thoughts to a greater power beyond my rational mind. Add to this a reclining chair that invites relaxation, and I'm "in Heaven." This is not only indulging my selfish appetites but is an attempt to get in touch with the mystical. Nor is the visual side of the experience paramount, as on rising in the dark, usually around 3:00 a.m., and sitting in the same office, I may experience a similar set of circumstances. In a sense I'm creating my own ashram peopled by images of those whom I admire most for their humanity and opening myself to the power of the Holy Spirit.

Even before my recent illness but because my cardiac condition precluded jogging or other common physical outlets, I began to jog on an indoor trampoline in my office. At first I tried a background of rhythmic or romantic music to help me to get my mind off mundane or stressful thoughts. On a hunch, I began to listen to a tape recording on one or another topic of New Age thinking I hoped would prove inspirational—such as an interview with Bede Griffiths. Success meant that I became completely absorbed in the topic and unaware of physical effort for about 30 minutes. Instead I experienced a feeling of exaltation and a gush of energy that may be similar to the high produced by the brain's endorphins when runners get their second wind, although in my case the stimulus appeared to be cerebral. Such experiences are probably commonplace, and everyone knows the thrill accompanying the grasp of a new concept. I well remember how, when I was nineteen in the student library at Edinburgh University, I read William James' (1961) *Varieties of Religious Experience* for the first time and decided that the mystical was the field I'd be most interested in eventually. In those days there seemed to be no choice but to finish medicine, and then start a training in psychiatry. This I did, but it was many years before I emerged from the orthodoxy of psychiatry and research to resume my quest for what lies beyond our ordinary conscious mind.

Hero worship was, I think, much more characteristic of my youth than is the case with adolescents today. This makes me sad, for the heroes represent tangible illustrations of an invisible God. An image based on first-hand experience seems to remain permanent, whereas those taken from literature or history may fade, having served their purpose at a particular state of one's development. In this context my involvement with Arthur Koestler, Aldous Huxley, and other outstanding humanists, has acted as an inspiration or as role models of seekers, and their deaths have not dimmed their images in any way. But the same applies to my family, who were equally important inspirational figures for me. In a different context, three of my girlfriends from university days more than 50 years ago are regular correspondents and we meet whenever possible even though two are behind the Iron Curtain.

As I contemplate in my "ashram," everyday rational thinking may give way to a more questioning state of mind, and I may see myself as a comparative stranger looking back at a life spent in treating patients and now wondering what this really means. I realize that my own deepest problems would not be solved by a therapist but would call for a new perspective of a deeper kind than would the rational or analytic approach. A higher level of consciousness is evoked that introduces a more holistic or global perspective, which diminishes the significance of my problem. I think of this twilight state as more related to my inner self than to my everyday rational self. It is a more abstract or egoless state of mind where I see that major problems are not solved, but outgrown. Such an awareness is accompanied by a feeling of immense relief. I remember critical visitors to our therapeutic communities in London or Melrose, where I worked for 12 and 7 years respectively, who always asked what treatment we used and who not infrequently left us convinced that we lacked a methodology that could be researched and subjected to reductive evaluation and ultimate proof.

INTEGRATION INTO THE WHOLE

Matthew Fox (1983), a Dominican priest and popular educator living in California, also demonstrates the tendency in recent years to see religion as an integral part of one's living a full and joyous life far removed from the doctrine of original sin. He calls this former, positive attitude Creation-Centered Spirituality, which he traces back to the 9th century B.C., and to the very beginnings of the Bible; whereas the latter attitude, the Fall/Redemption spiritual tradition, goes back principally to St. Augustine (354—430 A.D.). This tradition "considers all nature 'fallen' and does not seek God in nature but inside the individual soul, it is not only silent toward science but hostile to it." (Fox, 1983, p. 11.) It was the idea of original sin, a concept unknown to Christ, which dominated religion in Europe for a thousand years and led to the persecution of "sinners," who dared to think for themselves. To Matthew Fox and his followers, Creation Spirituality is a community of people building something together and integrating all the positive aspects of science, art, and religion for the betterment of man. This means that for Fox there is no problem in linking religion with the subatomic theory of the physicists or with the complexities of evolution, holograms, right and left hemispheres of the brain and their predominant characteristics, and so on. Ultimately it raises the question of our objective or rational view of reality as opposed to an inner or universal reality of which everyone is a part—what Carl Jung called the universal consciousness.

At a more subjective level, I have found that as I am more free to contemplate the universe we live in, it becomes ever more difficult to understand it in the reductive scientific or logical sense, and we have instead to conceptualize the idea of a truth, which we feel and know but cannot prove, as in the case of God. Once this freedom from the strict demand for proof is established, we are free to reassess the meaning of intuition in our lives and ask why fantasies, daydreams, fairy tales, and so on were pushed aside at school in order to prepare us for the real world of materialist striving and objective observation.

It occurs to me that there is a hint of second childhood in my present position. The relative credulity, the concession that anything is possible, that a paradigm may be an intelligent compromise between proof and the truth—all have something reminiscent of a youthful optimism and open-mindedness. In fact this trend may not reflect an aspect of senility but rather be an attitude of the wisdom of old age. In this context I can talk freely about some of the phenomena that I've become aware of in recent years.

In line with my growing interest in the spiritual part of self as described in previous chapters, I have begun to experience an occasional mystical event. For instance, two years ago in Rome I was attending Mass in St. Peter's with my wife. There was a superb black choir from the Caribbean, which was truly up-lifting. I stood looking immediately behind the altar at a stained glass window depicting a dove. I felt strangely drawn to this image, which slowly changed to an unmistakeable picture of the

Virgin Mary. This picture lasted for at least five minutes and left me with a feeling of exaltation and joy. I shared my experience with my wife as we were leaving St. Peter's. I was well aware of the symbol of the dove of peace, but vague about its connection with Mary, whom I only later learned is known to Catholics as the Queen of Peace. What does this experience prove? Nothing, you can say. Then why the feeling of exaltation and the rush of energy that lasted for hours? Influenced by my reading and openmindedness to such events, I feel I was part of an awareness beyond self and our five senses, time, and space, which make up our objective reason. I see it as a part of an extended consciousness or universal consciousness that which encompasses us all. I even feel when I'm writing an account like this that I am not under direct control of my cerebral cortex and am not my familiar thinking self. At times it almost amounts to automatic writing.

In Chapter 3 I gave another example of a mystical experience; in this instance a "state of grace" affecting a group of 29 people, mostly staff from drug units in various parts of Italy and beyond. After almost 30 hours covering a period of five days of intensive interaction, suddenly we had an intense silence lasting minutes. We were so overawed by the presence that the meeting broke up in complete silence. The training group had run out of time, but people were too moved to say farewells or thank yous. I walked outside and, alone in a nearby garden, wept tears of joy—a unique experience for me. In this instance the myth of absolute proof seemed irrelevant, as in retrospect everyone confirmed the awesome presence, while differing on the identity ascribed to the presence. For most of the group it was some aspect of God.

As is well known, our use of words is determined by our objective awareness of things, and we lack a vocabulary to describe mystical or paranormal phenomena. Even a word such as *mystical* causes problems of understanding. Spangler (1984) restricts the term to the discovery of the spirit of God within

oneself. He separates it from the word *religion*, which deals
with external acts of worship and behavior. This dichotomy
between objectively observable facts and subjectively experienced feelings is an important aspect of *process*, a word used
extensively throughout this book. Like the word "truth" it
cannot be a goal in itself. The *seeking* and not the *thing seen* is
what is important. If we try to objectify the process by describ-
ing an outcome of an insight or absolute truth, then we are
subverting the quality of process, as though transforming it
to an objective reality. In this negative sense we can equate
process with psychodynamics in psychology, but they have a
totally different significance.

ATMOSPHERE AND ATTITUDE IN THE PROCESS
OF CHANGE

Considerations such as these are at the heart of this book
about growing old—the ultimate freedom. If we seek answers
to the meaning of life exclusively at an objective level, we will
remain earthbound, seeing the world in unidimensional proportions and never finding answers that satisfy. Concepts such as
original sin torture many dying people, who desperately seek
forgiveness instead of looking for what Fox (1983) prefers to
call "original blessing" or love. He refers to the Native American use of the word *wisdom*—that people may live, which
implies beauty, joyousness, freedom of choice, and love of life.

My old age has been transformed positively by some such
process. My medical training conditioned me to believe in the
need for objective proof. From this I progressed to an uncertain
belief in the dogma of psychoanalysis where the analyst's
insights about the cause of patients' conflicts were considered as
though they amounted to objective truths reflecting the analyst's
unique wisdom and ignoring innumerable other factors in the
environment. Luckily for me I was at the beginning of my

community psychiatry experience at that time and found it necessary to repudiate three years of daily-training interviews by my training analyst. Gradually, the environment, associated with community work, proceeded to take precedence over the intrapsychic. For the past 40 years this process of growth has been evolving in a social environment ideal for such a metamorphosis. A social system run on democratic lines, such as a therapeutic community, has built-in checks and balances so that the abuse of authority, manipulative tactics, inaccurate or biased information, and the other bureaucratic practices familiar to us can be countered. Above all, process is seen as the top priority—not objective goals. This allows a flexibility that is largely impossible in most industries or academic institutions, where standardized employee training and strict guidelines supported by research data set everyone working toward a specific goal.

A frightening alternative to a democratic system called Krone training has recently appeared in industry. This approach is the brainchild of Werner Erhard, who in the 1970s developed a community health program known as EST, which became immensely popular with the general public. Krone training, used by many famous U.S. firms, including 67,000 employees of California's Pacific Bell, claims success as a result of achieving employee cohesion by developing a system of beliefs based on the teachings of a controversial philosopher and mystic. It is said that Pacific Bell had planned to spend $147 million of subscribers' money on Krone training.

To me, this whole approach to corporate profit defies belief. It is the opposite of an open social system, imposing the authority of obscure theoreticians through a gullible management onto their passive, dependent employees. I feel strongly about this social injustice, particularly having demonstrated in the *Process of Change* (Jones, 1982) that in an optimal environment for change it took as long as seven years to achieve a democratic social system that involved everyone in a process of growth.

HOLISTIC HUMOR

The concept of process as outlined above can almost be predicted to lead away from largely material considerations in favor of a more spiritual perspective. While it may seem irrelevant to many people, I feel that humor has a place in the process of change.

I find as I grow older that I am increasingly drawn to paradox and humor. Humor is in part the collision of consistent but incompatible ideas (Koestler, 1975)—like the English lady who, when asked about her husband's whereabouts, replied that he was enjoying eternal bliss but added, "I wish you wouldn't talk about such unpleasant subjects." Laughter in such circumstances is entirely spontaneous and results in a relief of tension and may even promote health as has been suggested by Cousins' *Anatomy of an Illness* (1979), wherein he attributes part of his recovery from a potentially fatal illness to this factor.

There seems to be a link between laughter, health, and creativity. Laughter often relieves tension and results in a state of well-being that may last all day. Suppose you are studying a complex subject such as quantum theory because you want to understand the expression "a quantum leap" in relation to the process of change. When the frustration associated with a difficult topic of study leads to understanding then the frustration gives way to a gush of satisfaction and relief and the energy released may last many hours and help to open the door for further understanding. This euphoria that follows the sudden understanding—when the intellect grasps the synthesis—is part of what we know as creativity and seems to have much in common with the mechanism of spontaneous laughter.

The comments above, applied to the aged, seem to have a special relevance. The typical retirement home, boarding home or nursing home is usually anything but a happy place. Where possible, we need to aim at an atmosphere of joyousness, laughter, understanding and creativity. In my experience as a psychiatrist in charge of a geriatric ward in a mental hospital, the staff and I, helped by the patients, met with considerable success (Jones, 1982).

Even the subject of death, discussed in the previous chapter, may have its humorous moments. Recently my wife and I were visiting some friends and, as it was getting late, I said to my wife, "You'd better take this old duffer home!" She replied, "I don't live with an old duffer, but you might." She's younger than I am and it seems that I'm forever apologizing for being old—a pointless gesture.

In a similar vein I tend to apologize about my evermore imminent demise and decided to visit the local mortician secretly in the hope of striking a bargain and sparing Chris some of the ugliness that inevitably surrounds funeral arrangements for the spouse. I'd done this successfully in the U.S.A. five or six years previously, where prices were exorbitant. I'd pushed the physician's bluff as though I knew all about burials and was no grief-stricken spouse ready to agree to anything—such as a more expensive coffin as a demonstration of love for the deceased. This worked beautifully—first, I wanted to be cremated, and wouldn't a strong cardboard box do? And second, I wanted to pay *now*. This cost me $500, which suited my Scottish parsimony fine! Unfortunately, I couldn't carry this bargain with me when we moved to Canada, but I did recover my $500.

I approached the appropriately forbidding-looking house and was confronted by a huge door, which I decided was meant for the pallbearers and their load, but no bell was visible. So I knocked timidly but the gloom remained unbroken. I went to the back of the house where to my relief some harmless vegetables were being delivered, and I was duly directed to the proper entrance. I was admitted by a grave, pale gentleman who politely invited me to enter. Again, I tried my bluff about a "bargain" funeral. The grave expression changed to a pained one and I was given to understand that this was no bargain basement and my whole approach was highly irregular if not irreverent. I tried to explain that it was *my* funeral, but somehow I was made to seem irrelevant. Chastened, I had to listen to how things happened "professionally" in Canada. For four months the ground was too hard for graves to be dug, but there were adequate cold-storage facilities. "But," I expostulated, "I want to be cremated." At this, the black-suited gentleman patiently explained that I, or rather my remains, had to be driven 60 miles to the nearest crematorium. I seemed to be getting nowhere and was relieved when a tired-looking elderly man in workclothes sat down subserviently nearby and said apologetically that the ground had become too hard to allow further digging. This obviously called for serious "professional" planning and I slipped away, feeling that my death, like so many things in real life, was of minor concern.

Maybe I was taking life (and death) too seriously, and when I told my wife we laughed heartily! Not at the grave news of a "bargain" that I'd intended, but rather a good laugh at my expense now seemed much healthier!

This topic of conversation was raised again a few nights later at the house of some friends. Again, I felt myself becoming too serious about the fuss we make over funerals and as though in compensation, the group described how my funeral party, after cremation, could be planned as a superlative binge, which in some mysterious way would cheer me up!

RISE OF SPIRITUALITY

I have associated creativity and spirituality as being initially present in early childhood and then being largely ignored by the adult world and education—to reappear at least in some people in old age. In addition, these attributes are commonly associated with native peoples in all parts of the world who have retained their simple beliefs in nature and an all-powerful god.

Western man has failed badly where religion is concerned, and in general would seem to have lost the early spirituality of biblical times, except perhaps in some monasteries and possibly some religious subgroups. The split between religion and the sciences over the last three centuries has not helped, and it has only confused most people as to where the truth lies. However, things are changing and it is significant that in Protestant seminaries today over half the seminarians are women. Not only that, but as I found in my group of university students, and as people are discovering everywhere, youth is demanding that more attention be paid to spirituality in places of learning and elsewhere.

In this context, Fritjof Capra (1975 & 1982) as well as Einstein and many other scientists, find mysticism in their fields of work. By showing that matter is alive, that time is not linear, and the Newtonian Laws of cause and effect to be no longer sufficient, they are bringing science, religion and psychology together after a gap of 300 years. To quote Capra:

> The mystical view of consciousness is based on the experience of reality in non-ordinary modes of awareness, which are traditionally achieved through meditation but may also occur spontaneously in the process of artistic creation and in various other contexts. Modern psychologists have come to call non-ordinary experiences of this kind "transpersonal" because they seem to allow the individual mind to make contact with collective and even cosmic mental patterns . . . the systems view of mind seems perfectly consistent with both the scientific and the mystical views of consciousness and thus to provide the ideal framework for unifying the two. (Capra, 1982, p. 297)

NEW AGE FOR OLD AGE: OUR PERSONAL GOALS

We tend to think of higher creativity or genius as something reserved for a few highly gifted people whom we can only admire or envy. There is a growing awareness that we may all have such latent potential, but that we reject the possibility without ever considering it seriously. It may be that the elderly in some instances, freed from the restraints of a routine job and caring less about appearances and the inhibitions imposed by our culture, are in a position to contemplate the meaning of life. If so, they may look inward and discover other more spiritual, intuitive, inspirational or creative ideas. This is certainly what is happening to me, and it is available, I believe, to anyone who is dedicated to such a search. Going on the assumption that the prior scramble associated with my active professional life drained most of my energy, I afterwards began to ask myself who I really was, as opposed to who I was expected to be according to my cultural environment. My children were grown up, my wife had her own career to pursue, and I was getting too old to be a teacher/consultant in my own particular field.

In my search for the spiritual over the last decade, and in my interest in transpersonal psychology linking mind and the collective unconscious, I myself have had relatively little success. As already stated in this chapter, I believe that everyone has this latent potential as manifested by our rich fantasy life in childhood, but to recover that capacity in old age or in any other age is certainly a challenge. We seem to be moving rapidly to a more open-minded attitude toward the immense significance and importance of intuition, inspiration, mysticism, and spirituality. In this sense, our culture in the West is leaving its rigid attitude toward an objective reality and countenancing the validity of the probable and the paradigm. Moreover, the emphasis on meditation as the main method to achieve subjective detachment from our objective environment is beginning to be joined by other possibilities.

In this connection, the age-old practice of shamanism, found at one time in all parts of the world, is arousing considerable interest. Michael Harner (1986), an anthropologist, has studied this phenomenon first-hand in various parts of the world. He argues most convincingly that their influence is beneficial to man and would have survived even in the West had it not been for the Church and the Inquisition, which could not tolerate other powerful Gods. His understanding of shamanism has enriched his own life and helped him relate to God and to recognize the awesome power of the universe and our indebtedness to ecology, as well as our closeness to animals, plants, and so on. Moreover, by using shamanistic drums and other methods, he can put people in touch with their spiritual selves, which for most of us are so tantalisingly elusive.

Another approach to this hidden part of mind beyond consciousness is described by Brother Charles, Director of the M.S.H. Foundation in Virginia. For 12 years he was very close to the famous Indian mystic, Muktananda, and became his personal secretary up to the time of the guru's death. Brother Charles, starting from the time-consuming meditative techniques he learned from his teacher, Muktananda, has become interested in the use of energy from sound to slow down brain-wave frequencies. Meditating monks who, after hours, reach a transcendental state, are linked up to an electroencephalogram (EEG) and show synchronized delta waves in both hemispheres of the brain. When Brother Charles uses volunteers and the use of special sound, the rapid-brain frequencies of the waking state can be slowed down within minutes to delta rhythm and become synchronized, thus simulating the meditating monks. The result appears to be very similar to the meditative state, and the mind is no longer active and subject to mental stress. In the process, the right and left brains are balanced and no longer in conflict, but this is not the place to discuss hemisphere dominance, which is a separate field of study.

There are many other areas of brain functioning where dramatic innovations are appearing at a remarkable rate. To mention one other new phenomenon, conscious dreaming is being studied by Stephen La Berge at Stanford, and by many other researchers. This is an attempt to tap another dimension of brain function outside everyday consciousness, with a view to tapping more of our latent brain potential. The author believes that in the dream state there is far more knowledge available than in the waking state and claims that this may result in better decision making and even in foreknowledge. In his opinion, out-of-body experiences and near-death experiences previously referred to in Chapter 4 can both be explained by what he calls *Lucid Dreaming*, the title of his book (La Berge, 1985).

Despite all the technological advances and researches like those just described, which are occurring with increasing frequency, self-study still remains fundamental if we are to see a more responsible world climate emerging before it is too late to avoid destruction by either the atomic bomb or our abuse of the natural environment. As is stressed throughout this book, we older people must set a standard for self-reflection, because we are in a favored position to do so. This is different from the concept of psychoanalysis, which is concerned with the elimination of ego defenses or with repressed memories. Nor is it the long-term goal of selflessness, as attained through the discipline of meditation. By turning one's attention inward and aspiring to achieve an open mind, allowing for contradictory or paradoxical thoughts, and, freed from the lifelong pressures of orthodoxy and educational conditioning, a new self may begin to appear—a self that is akin to a subliminal consciousness. Such a process might be reinforced in contemplative environments like those found in Bede Griffith's ashram in Southern India, or in one of the many creative settings such as Esalen in California or Findhorn in Scotland—but it is still the subjective awareness that matters most.

It is this self-awareness that has been largely lost in our Western world, and that must be regained if we are to rediscover our lost potential. Surely we must try to tune in to the impressions and feelings all around us that we tend to ignore; whereas, the shaman chooses to talk to the trees, plants, and animals—and even to the rocks. This self-awareness opens our minds to the wider field of intuition and to our latent ability to get beyond the reality of the scientific rational world in order to find a new reality in spiritual experiences, intuition, and the mystery of life itself. We are still only vaguely aware of this need to search for the truth if we are to escape from the illusion we call reality. The need to find a deeper reality—which most of us have only sensed momentarily if at all—is the major theme of this book and, I believe, a major purpose of life.

Bibliography

A course of miracles. (1981). Tiburon, CA: Foundation for Inner Peace.

Argyris, C. (1970). *Intervention theory and method.* Reading, MA: Addison-Wesley.

Bateson, M.C. (1980). *CoEvolution Quarterly, 28,* Six Days of Dying, p. 4–11.

Bolen, J.S. (1979). *The tao of psychology.* San Francisco: Harper & Row.

Brain/Mind Bulletin. (1986). *12*(2).

Brain/Mind Bulletin. (1987). *12*(7).

Campbell, J. (1972). *Myths to live by.* New York: Viking.

Capra, F. (1975). *The tao of physics.* London: Flamingo Press.

Capra, F. (1982). *The turning point.* New York: Simon & Schuster.

Cousins, Norman. (1979). *Anatomy of an illness.* New York: Norton.

Deikman, A.J. (1982). *The observing self.* Boston: Beacon Press.

du Boulay, S. (1984). *Cicely Saunders.* London: Hodder & Stoughton.

Ferguson, M. (1980). *The Aquarian conspiracy.* Los Angeles: Tarcher.

Fox, M. (1983). *Original blessing.* New Mexico: Bear & Co.

Garfield, C., & Bennett, H.Z. (1984). *Peak performers—The new heroes of american business.* Los Angeles: Tarcher.

Griffiths, B. (1982). *The marriage of east and west.* London: Collins.

Griffiths, B. (1983). *The cosmic revelation.* Springfield, IL: Templegate.

Harman, N., & Rheingold, H. (1984). *Higher creativity.* Los Angeles: Tarcher.

Harner, M. (1986). *The way of the shaman.* New York: Bantam Books.

James, W. (1961). *The varieties of religious experience.* New York: Collier Macmillan.

Jampolsky, G.G. (1985). *Goodbye to guilt.* New York: Bantam Books.

Jones, M. (1952). *Social psychiatry: A study of therapeutic communities.* London: Tavistock.

Jones, M. (1962). *Social psychiatry: In the community, in hospitals and in prisons.* Springfield, IL: Charles C. Thomas.

Jones, M. (1968a). *Beyond the therapeutic community: Social learning and social psychiatry.* New Haven: Yale University Press.

Jones, M. (1968b). *Social psychiatry in practice.* London: Penguin.

Jones, M. (1974). Psychiatry, systems theory, education and change. *British Journal of Psychiatry, 124,* 75–80.

Jones, M. (1976). *Maturation of the therapeutic community.* New York: Human Sciences Press.

Jones, M. (1980). Desirable features of a therapeutic community in a prison. In Hans Toch (Ed.), *Therapeutic communities in corrections,* (pp. 34–40). New York: Praeger.

Jones, M. (1982). *The process of change.* London: Routledge & Kegan Paul.

Jones, M. (1986). Therapeutic communities (open systems) and a global system for change. *International Journal of Therapeutic Communities, 7*(4), p. 277–283.

Jones, M., & Stanford, G. (1973, November). *Phi Delta Kappan,* p. 201–224.

Jung, C.G. (1951). *On synchronicity.* Collected works, (Vol. 8.) New Jersey: Princeton University Press.

Jung, C.G. (1965). *Memories, dreams and reflections*. New York: Random House/Vintage.

Kenworthy, L.S. (1969). *Sixteen Quaker leaders speak*. Richmond, IN: Friends United Press.

Koestler, A. (1975). *The act of creation*. London: Picador.

Krishnamurti, J., & Bohm, D. (1985). *The ending of time*. San Francisco: Harper & Row.

Kubler-Ross, E. (1969). *On death and dying*. New York: Macmillan.

La Berge, S. (1985). *Lucid dreaming*. Los Angeles: Tarcher.

Luce, Gay. (1979). *Your second life*. New York: Delacorte Press/ Seymour Lawrence.

MacLaine, S. (1983). *Out on a limb*. New York: Bantam.

Maslow, A. (1964). *Religions, values, peak experiences*. New York: Viking.

Moody, R.A. (1975). *Life after life*. Atlanta: Mockingbird Books.

Moss, R.M. (1981). *The I that is we*. Berkeley: Celestial Arts.

Needleman, Jacob. (1980). *Lost Christianity*. San Francisco: Harper & Row.

Novak, M. (1985). *Successful aging*. New York: Penguin.

Roszak, T. (1978). *Person/planet*. New York: Anchor Press/Doubleday.

Roszak, T. (1987). *The cult of information*. Toronto: Random Press.

Sheldrake, R. (1981). *A New Science of Life*. Los Angeles: Tarcher.

Spangler, D. (1984). *Emergence—The rebirth of the sacred*. New York: Dell.

Szasz, T. (1974). *The myth of mental illness*. New York: Harper & Row.

Wilber, K. (Ed.). (1982). *The holographic paradigm*. London: Shambhala.

Ziegenfuss, J.T. (1983). *Patients' rights and organizational models*. Washington, DC: University Press of America.

Zukav, G. (1979). *The dancing Wu Li masters*. London: Bantam Books.

Index